Introduction

When I started freesciencelessons in 2013, I had one simple goal[...] [...] their understanding of science. When I was at school (and we're talk[...] years ago now), science was always my favourite subject. It's not surprising [...]at I went on to become a science teacher. I know that many students find science challenging. But I really believe that this doesn't have to be the case. With patient teaching and a bit of hard work, any student can make amazing progress.

Back in 2013, I had no idea how big freesciencelessons would become. The channel now has nearly 70 million views from 192 countries with a total view time of over 300 years. I love to hear from the students who have patiently watched the videos and realised that they can do science after all, despite in many cases having little confidence in their ability. And just like in 2013, I still make all the videos myself (many students think that I have a staff of helpers, but no, it's just me).

This workbook is designed to complement the Physics 2 videos for the AQA specification. However, there is a huge amount of overlap with other exam boards and in the future I'll be making videos and workbooks for those as well. I've packed the workbook full of questions to help you with your science learning. You might decide to start at the beginning and answer every question in the book or you might prefer to dip in and out of chapters depending on what you want to learn. Either way is fine. I've also written very detailed answers for every question, again to help you really develop your understanding. You can find these by scanning the QR code on the front of the book or by visiting freesciencelessons.co.uk/p2tv1

Please don't think of science as some sort of impossible mountain to climb. Yes there are some challenging bits but it's not as difficult as people think. Take your time, work hard and believe in yourself. When you find a topic difficult, don't give up. Just go to a different topic and come back to it later.

Finally, if you have any feedback on the workbooks, you're welcome to let me know (support@freesciencelessons.co.uk). I'm always keen to make the workbooks better so if you have a suggestion, I'd love to hear it.

Good luck on your journey. I hope that you get the grades that you want.

Shaun Donnelly

Revision Tips

The first important point about revision is that you need to be realistic about the amount of work that you need to do. Essentially you have to learn two years of work (or three if you start GCSEs in Year 9). That's a lot of stuff to learn. So give yourself plenty of time. If you're very serious about getting a top grade then I would recommend starting your revision as early as you can. I see a lot of messages on Youtube and Twitter from students who leave their revision until the last minute. That's their choice but I don't think it's a good way to get the best grades.

To revise successfully for any subject (but I believe particularly for science), you have to really get into it. You have to get your mind deep into the subject. That's because science has some difficult concepts that require thought and concentration. So you're right in the middle of that challenging topic and your phone pings. Your friend has sent you a message about something that he saw on Netflix. You reply and start revising again. Another message appears. This is from a different friend who has a meme they want to share. And so on and so on.

What I'm trying to tell you is that successful revision requires isolation. You need to shut yourself away from distractions and that includes your phone. Nothing that any of your friends have to say is so critically important that it cannot wait until you have finished. Just because your friends are bored does not mean that your revision has to suffer. Again, it's about you taking control.

Remember to give yourself breaks every now and then. You'll know when it's time. I don't agree with people who say you need a break every fifteen minutes (or whatever). Everyone is different and you might find that your work is going so well that you don't need a break. In that case don't take one. If you're taking breaks every ten minutes then the question I would ask is do you need them? Or are you trying to avoid work?

There are many different ways to revise and you have to find what works for you. I believe that active revision is the most effective. I know that many students like to copy out detailed notes (often from my videos). Personally, I don't believe that this is a great way to revise since it's not really active. A better way is to watch a video and then try to answer the questions from this book. If you can't, then you might want to watch the video again (or look carefully at the answers to check the part that you struggled with).

The human brain learns by repetition. So the more times that you go over a concept, the more fixed it will become in your brain. That's why revision needs so much time, because you really need to go over everything more than once (ideally several times) before the exam.

Revision Tips

I find with my students that flashcards are a great way to learn facts. Again, that's because the brain learns by repetition. My students write a question on one side and the answer on the other. They then practise them until they've memorised the answer. I always advise them to start by memorising five cards and then gradually adding in extra cards, rather than try to memorise fifty cards at once.

I've noticed over the last few years that more students do past paper practise as a way of revising. I do not recommend this at all. A past paper is what you do AFTER you have revised. Imagine that you are trying to learn to play the guitar. So you buy a guitar and rather than having lessons, you book yourself into a concert hall to give a performance. And you keep giving performances until you can play. Would you recommend that as a good strategy? I wouldn't. But essentially that's how lots of students try to revise. Yes by all means do practise papers (I've included a specimen paper in this book for you) but do them at the end when you've done all your revision. Past papers require you to pull lots of different bits of the specification together, so you should only do them when you are capable of that (ie when you've already done loads of revision).

A couple of final points ....

To reduce our environmental impact and to keep the price of this book reasonable, the answers are available online. Simply scan the QR code on the front or visit www.freesciencelessons.co.uk/p2tv1

There will be times when I decide to update a book, for example to make something clearer or maybe to correct a problem (I hope not many of those). So please keep an eye out for updates. I'll post them on Twitter (@UKscienceguy) and also on the FAQ page of my website. If you think that you've spotted a mistake or a problem, please feel free to contact me.

Copyright information: The copyright of this workbook belongs to Shaun Donnelly. Copying of this workbook is strictly prohibited. Anyone found in breach of copyright will be prosecuted.

Physics Equation Sheet

Word Equation	Symbol Equation	Higher Only
elastic potential energy = 0.5 x spring constant x (extension)^2	$E_e = \dfrac{1}{2} k e^2$	
change in thermal energy = mass x specific heat capacity x temperature change	$\Delta E = m\, c\, \Delta\theta$	
thermal energy for a change of state = mass x specific latent heat	$E = m L$	
For gases: pressure x volume = constant	$p V = $ constant	
pressure due to a column of liquid = height of column x density of liquid x gravitational field strength (g)	$p = h \rho g$	Yes
(final velocity)^2 - (initial velocity)^2 = 2 x acceleration x distance	$v^2 - u^2 = 2as$	
force = $\dfrac{\text{change in momentum}}{\text{time taken}}$	$F = \dfrac{m\Delta v}{\Delta t}$	Yes
period = $\dfrac{1}{\text{frequency}}$	$T = \dfrac{1}{f}$	
magnification = $\dfrac{\text{image height}}{\text{object height}}$		
force on a conductor (at right angles to a magnetic field) carrying a current = magnetic flux density x current x length	$F = B I l$	Yes
$\dfrac{\text{potential difference across primary coil}}{\text{potential difference across secondary coil}} = \dfrac{\text{number of turns in primary coil}}{\text{number of turns in secondary coil}}$	$\dfrac{V_p}{V_s} = \dfrac{n_p}{n_s}$	Yes
potential difference across primary coil x current in primary coil = potential difference across secondary coil x current in secondary coil	$V_p I_p = V_s I_s$	Yes

Contents

Contents

Contents

Contents

Chapter 1: Forces

- Describe the differences between scalar and vector quantities and give examples of these quantities.

- Describe what is meant by a contact force and a non-contact force and give examples of these types of forces.

- Describe the difference between mass and weight and explain how weight can be determined using a calibrated spring balance (newton meter).

- Determine the weight of an object given its mass and calculate the gravitational field strength from mass and weight data.

- Describe what is meant by a resultant force and calculate the resultant force of forces acting in a parallel direction.

- Draw free body diagrams to show the forces acting on an object.

- Construct vector diagrams to determine the resultant force produced by forces acting an angle.

- Construct scale diagrams to resolve a force into horizontal and vertical components.

- Describe the energy transfers taking place when forces act.

- Calculate the work done by a force.

- Describe the possible effects of forces on elastic objects.

- Calculate the force required to extend or compress an elastic object.

- Describe how to carry out the required practical to investigate the effect of force on the extension of a spring.

- Calculate the moment produced by a force.

- Carry out calculations based on balanced moments.

- Explain how a force can cause an object to topple.

- Describe how levers are force multipliers and carry out calculations based on levers.

- Describe how gears can be used to increase or decrease the turning effect of a force.

- Calculate the pressure in a fluid and explain why the density of the Earth's atmosphere decreases with altitude.

Chapter 1 : Forces

- Describe what is meant by upthrust and explain why certain objects float or sink in liquids based on their density.

- Explain how speed is a scalar quantity and carry out calculations to determine the speed of a moving object.

- Explain how velocity is a vector quantity and carry out calculations to determine the velocity of a moving object.

- Construct a distance-time graph to show the journey of an object moving in a straight line.

- Determine the speed of an object from a distance-time graph.

- Calculate the acceleration of an object.

- Construct a velocity-time graph to show the journey of an object.

- Use a velocity-time graph to determine the acceleration of an object and the total distance travelled by the object.

- Describe how the velocity of an object changes as it moves through a fluid and explain why an object reaches terminal velocity.

- Describe Newton's First Law of Motion and use this law to explain how forces affect the motion of an object.

- Describe Newton's Second Law of Motion and calculate the acceleration of an object caused by a resultant force.

- Describe Newton's Third Law of Motion.

- Describe how the velocity of a skydiver changes due to the forces acting.

- Describe how to carry out the required practical on acceleration.

- Describe the factors that influence the stopping distance of a vehicle.

- Calculate the energy changes taking place when a vehicle brakes.

- Calculate the momentum of a moving object.

- Describe how momentum is conserved and use the idea of conservation of momentum to calculate the velocity or mass of objects.

- Calculate the forces involved during momentum changes.

- Describe how safety features can reduce the risk of injury due to momentum change.

Scalar and Vector Quantities

. Quantities in Physics are either scalar quantities or vector quantities.

. Complete the box below to show the features of scalar and vector quantities.

Scalar quantities only have a magnitude. Scalar quantities do not have a _____.

Unlike scalar quantities, _____ quantities have both a magnitude and a direction.

. What is meant by the word "magnitude"?

Distance is a scalar quantity but displacement is a vector quantity.

he diagram shows some of the towns which are a distance of 30 km om Birmingham.

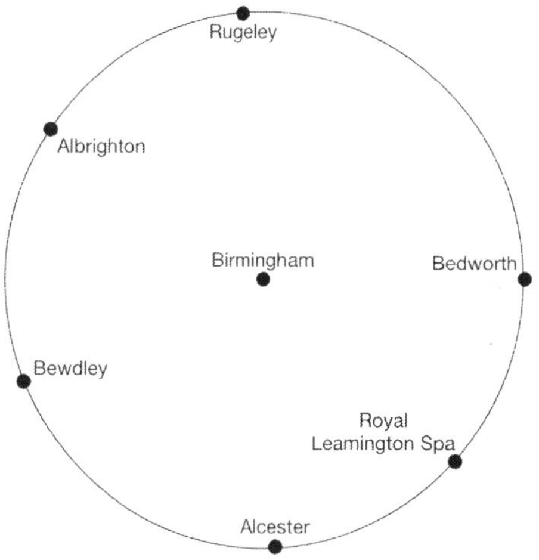

Explain why "a distance of 30 km from Birmingham" is a scalar quantity.

Identify the town which is "a displacement of 30 km due East of rmingham" and explain why this is a vector quantity.

Represent the vector in question b as an arrow on the map.

The quantities below are either scalars or vectors.

rite "S" for scalar quantities and "V" for vector quantities.

Mass	Acceleration	Momentum	Distance	Speed	Weight

Force	Temperature	Velocity	Displacement	Time	Energy

a. The arrow shows a force of 20 N acting wnwards.

aw another arrow to show a force of 40 N acting wards.

3 b. The arrows below represent displacement.

The top arrow shows a displacement of 100 m due East.

What is shown by the bottom arrow?

Contact and Non-Contact Forces

1. Forces explain many of the effects that we see in Physics.

Complete the sentences below by using the correct words from the list.

magnitude	**contact**	**vector**	**shape**	**pull**	**direction**	**interacts**

A force is a push or a _____ experienced when one object _____ with

another object. Forces can change the speed or _____ that an object moves. Forces ca[n]

also change an object's _____ . Because forces have _____ (size) and

direction, this means that forces are _____ quantities. The unit of force is the newton (N[)].

A _____ force can take place when objects are touching. If the objects experience a

force when they are not touching, then this is an example of a non-contact force.

2. There are four examples of contact forces.

These are friction, tension, air resistance and normal contact force.

The diagrams below show examples of these types of forces.

In each case, identify the type of force involved and the objects in contact.

Sliding down playground slide

Type of force =

Objects in contact =

Tug of war

Type of force =

Objects in contact =

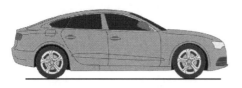

Stationary car on road

Type of force =

Objects in contact =

Skydiver

Type of force =

Objects in contact =

There are three main examples of non-contact forces.

These are gravitational force, electrostatic force and magnetic force.

Draw lines between the correct boxes to show the features of these types of force.

| Gravitational Force | This force can attract or repel | This force acts between objects which have a charge | Two magnetic North poles |

| Electrostatic Force | This is always an attractive force | This force acts between magnets and certain objects | A satellite and the Earth |

| Magnetic Force | This force can attract or repel | This force acts between all objects | Two positive particles |

The following statements all concern different types of forces.

Decide which of the statements are true and which of the statements are false.

Rewrite the false statements correctly in the space below.

A force can only change the speed
of an object

True / False

The force between a book and a
desk is normal contact force

True / False

Gravitational force is a contact force
because the two objects must be touching

True / False

Non-contact forces are scalar quantities
because they do not have a direction

True / False

Non-contact forces are always
forces of attraction

True / False

Electrostatic forces can act
between any charged objects

True / False

Gravity and Weight

1. The mass of a typical family car is around 1000 kg.

a. What will be the mass of this car in the following locations?

The Earth	The Moon	Mars
Mass of car =	Mass of car =	Mass of car =

b. Complete the sentences below by circling the correct words.

The mass / weight of an object tells us the amount of matter in the object.

The mass / weight does not depend on where the object is.

2. The weight of an object is the force acting on it due to gravity.

a. Explain why the unit of weight is the newton (N).

b. We can measure the weight of an object using a calibrated spring balance (also called a newtonmeter).

The diagram shows newtonmeters weighing different masses.

Plot the readings from the newtonmeters on the graph.

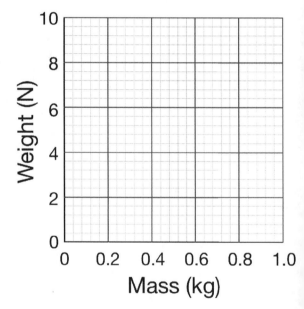

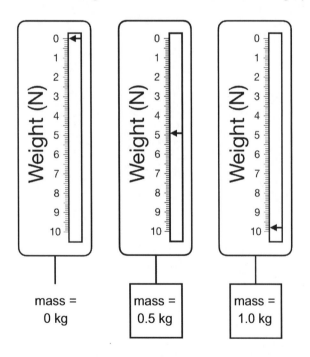

mass = 0 kg

mass = 0.5 kg

mass = 1.0 kg

c. The weight of an object is directly proportional to the object's mass.

This is written as: weight ∝ mass

What is meant by the symbol ∝ ?

d. Explain how the graph shows that the weight of an object is directly proportional to the object's mass.

You are not give the equation for weight in the exam so you need to learn it.

| Weight (N) | = | Mass (kg) | X | Gravitational field strength (N / kg) |

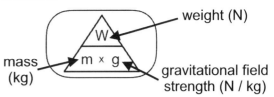

Calculate the weight of an object with a mass of 2.5 kg on the surface of the Earth.
The value of g on the surface of the Earth is 9.8 N / kg.

Calculate the weight of the same object on the surface of Mars.
The value of g on the surface of Mars is 3.8 N / kg.

Calculate the weight of an object with a mass of 750 g on the surface of the Moon.
The value of g on the surface of the Moon is 1.6 N / kg.

An object with a mass of 5 kg has a weight of 44 N on the surface of Venus.
Calculate the value of g on the surface of Venus.

An object has a weight of 54 N on the surface of Mercury.
Calculate the mass of the object.
The value of g on the surface of Mercury is 3.6 N / kg.

In every object, there is a single point where the weight (ie the force due to gravity) is considered to act.
What name do scientists give to this point?

| Centre of gravity | Centre of mass | Centre of force |

Resultant Forces

1. The diagram shows a person accelerating upwards in a lift.

The arrows show the forces acting.

a. Calculate the resultant force acting on the lift and the person.

(Remember that force is a vector and requires a direction).

Tension force of cable = 8000 N

Weight of lift and person = 6000 N

b. Draw a single arrow on the diagram to show the resultant force.

c. Complete the free body diagram below.

Remember that a free body diagram shows the individual forces, not the resultant force.

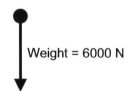

Weight = 6000 N

2. The diagram shows a skydiver moving towards the ground.

The arrows show the forces acting.

a. Calculate the resultant force acting on the skydiver.

Air resistance = 1000 N

Weight of skydiver and parachute = 800 N

b. Draw a single arrow on the diagram to show the resultant force.

c. Complete the free body diagram below.

The diagram shows a stationary van.

The arrows show the forces acting.

Complete the free body diagram for the van.

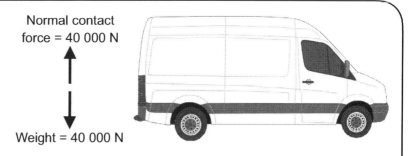

Normal contact
force = 40 000 N

Weight = 40 000 N

Calculate the resultant force acting on the van.

The diagram shows an airplane flying at a constant speed and a constant altitude.

The arrows show the forces acting.

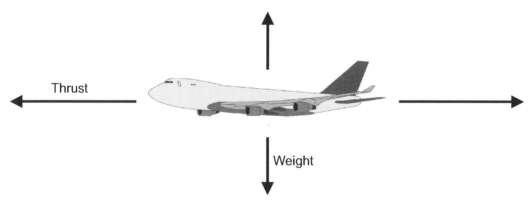

Thrust

Weight

What is meant by the word altitude?

Name the upwards force acting on the airplane.

What is meant by "thrust"?

Complete the free body diagram for the airplane.

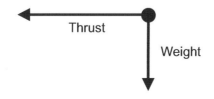

Thrust

Weight

Vector Diagrams

Exam tip: If you are asked to draw a vector diagram in the exam, make your diagram as large as possible. This increases the accuracy of your final answer.

1. Complete the sentences below by using the correct words from the list.

larger　　　**effect**　　　**smaller**　　　**parallel**　　　**resultant**　　　**object**

When several forces are acting on an _____ , we could replace all of the forces with

a single force which has the same _____ . Scientists call this single force the

_____ force. If the forces are acting in _____ to each other then

we simply subtract the _____ force from the _____ force.

2. When forces are acting at an angle, we find the resultant force by constructing a vector diagram.

Complete the vector diagrams below to work out the resultant force produced by the forces shown.

a. In the diagram below, 1 cm = 10 N.

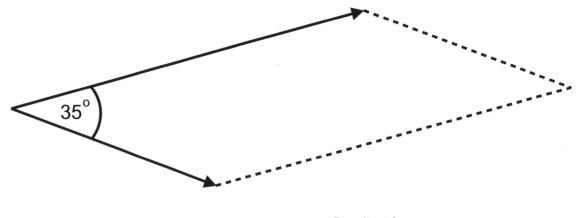

Resultant force = _____ N

b. In the diagram below, 1 cm = 30 N.

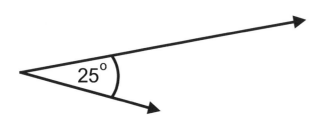

Resultant force = _____ N

Construct vector diagrams to determine the resultant force produced by the forces described.

You will need to select your scale in each case.

A 3 N force and a 4 N force are acting on an object.

The angle between the forces is 40°.

Resultant force = _____ N

A 1500 N force and a 1200 N force are acting on an object.

The angle between the forces is 50°.

Resultant force = _____ N

Two forces act on an object.

300 N force acts horizontally (rightwards) and a 200 N force acts vertically (upwards).

Determine the angle of the resultant force from the horizontal.

Resultant force = _____ N   Angle from horizontal = _____ °

Resolving Forces

1. The diagrams below show three forces.

a. Draw lines to link each force to the correct description.

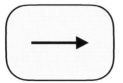

This force acts in both the horizontal and vertical directions.

y component only

This force acts only in the horizontal direction. No part of this force acts in the vertical direction.

x component only

This force acts only in the vertical direction. No part of this force acts in the horizontal direction.

Both x and y components

b. The diagrams below show two forces acting diagonally.

Resolve each force into its components in the horizontal and vertical directions.

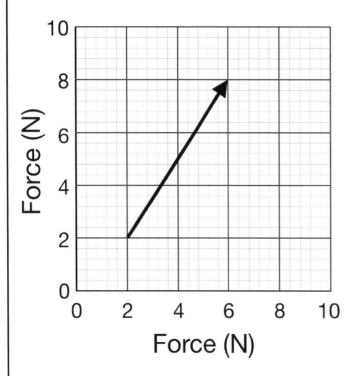

horizontal
component = _____ N

vertical
component = _____ N

horizontal
component = _____ N

vertical
component = _____ N

300 N force is acting at an angle of 25° to the horizontal.

ng the space below, determine the horizontal and vertical components of this force.

horizontal
component = _____ N

vertical
component = _____ N

10 N force is acting at an angle of 20° to the horizontal.

ng the space below, determine the horizontal and vertical components of this force.

horizontal
component = _____ N

vertical
component = _____ N

Work Done and Energy Transfer

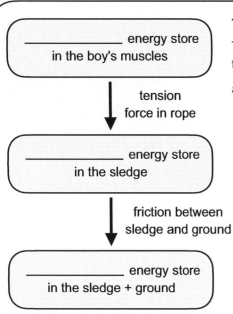

_____ energy store
in the boy's muscles

↓ tension
force in rope

_____ energy store
in the sledge

↓ friction between
sledge and ground

_____ energy store
in the sledge + ground

1. The diagram below shows a boy dragging a sledge along the ground.

The horizontal component of the force causes the sledge to move along the surface of the ground.

a. Complete the boxes to show the energy transfers taking place.

b. The boy dragging a sledge is an example of work done.

Fill in the gaps below to show what is meant by work done.

Work done is when a _____ is used to move an object.

Work done is an example of _____ transfer.

2. You are not given the equation for work done in the exam so you need to learn it.

Work done = Force × Distance along line of
(J)   (N)   action of force (m)

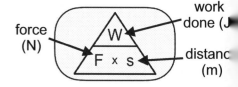

a. Which of the following is another unit for work done?

Circle one box.

watt   newton-metre   newton

b. Look again at question 1.

The boy is applying a horizontal force of 15 N to drag the sledge.

He drags the sledge a distance of 8 m.

Calculate the work done by the boy dragging the sledge.

work done = _____ J

A driver applies the brakes of her car.

The braking force is 4500 N.

The car comes to a complete stop in 20 m.

Calculate the work done by the brakes.

work done = _____ J

Explain why the temperature of the brakes increases.

Later, the car brakes again. This time the work done is 25 000 J.

The car takes 50 m to come to a complete stop.

Calculate the braking force of the car.

braking force = _____ N

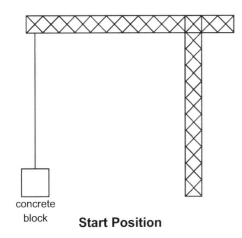

concrete
block   **Start Position**

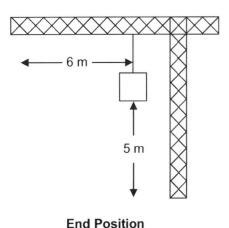

← 6 m →

5 m

End Position

4. A crane is used to lift a concrete block.

The weight of the block acts downwards.

The diagram shows the start and final positions of the crane.

a. The concrete block has a mass of 500 kg.

Calculate the weight of the block (the gravitational field strength at the surface of the Earth is 9.8 N / kg).

weight = _____ N

b. The block moves a vertical distance of 5 m and a horizontal distance of 6 m.

Calculate the work done in moving the concrete block.

work done = _____ J

Forces and Elasticity

1. Many materials are elastic or inelastic.

The diagram shows forces being applied to a stationary object.

a. What type of material is shown in the diagram?

> elastic material

> inelastic material

b. Explain how the diagram shows this.

c. The forces acting on the object are balanced.

How can we tell this from the arrows?

Forces applied

Forces removed

d. Complete the diagrams below to show what would happen to the same object with the forces applied.

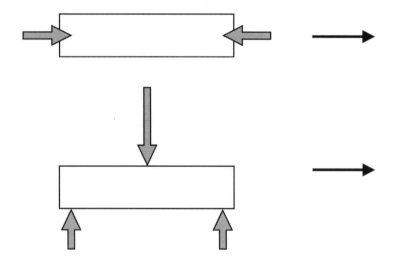

e. Complete the sentences about elastic and inelastic materials.

> An _____ material returns to its original shape when forces are removed.
>
> An _____ material does not return to its original shape when forces are removed.

f. In all of the examples above, more than one force is being applied to a stationary object.

What would happen to the stationary object if only one force is applied?

Explain your answer.

. We can calculate the force needed to stretch or compress an object using the equation below.

ou are not given this equation in the exam so you need to learn it.

emember that the equation also applies to compression as well as extension.

| Force (N) | = | Spring constant (N / m) | x | Extension (m) |

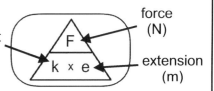

spring constant (N / m)

force (N)

extension (m)

A material has a length of 0.5 m and a spring constant of 50 N / m.

tretching forces are applied and the object increases in length to 1 m.

alculate the force required for this extension.

Force = _____ N

A material has a length of 0.2 m and a spring constant of 80 N / m.

ompression forces are applied and the object decreases in length to 0.1 m.

alculate the force required for this compression.

Force = _____ N

20 N of stretching force are applied to a material.

ie length of the material increases by 0.1 m.

alculate the spring constant for the material.

Spring constant = _____ N / m

Complete the sentences below by selecting the correct words from the boxes.

hen a person stretches or compresses an elastic object,

| thermal energy |
| chemical energy |
| elastic potential energy |

stores in the person's

uscles transfer to the

| elastic potential energy |
| kinetic energy |
| thermal energy |

store in the elastic object. This is an example of work done.

ie total work done is

| greater than |
| less than |
| equal to |

the energy transferred as long as the object is not inelastically deformed.

Required Practical: Stretching a Spring

1. In this required practical we will investigate how a force affects the extension of a spring.

a. The diagram shows the equipment used.

Label the diagram using the labels below.

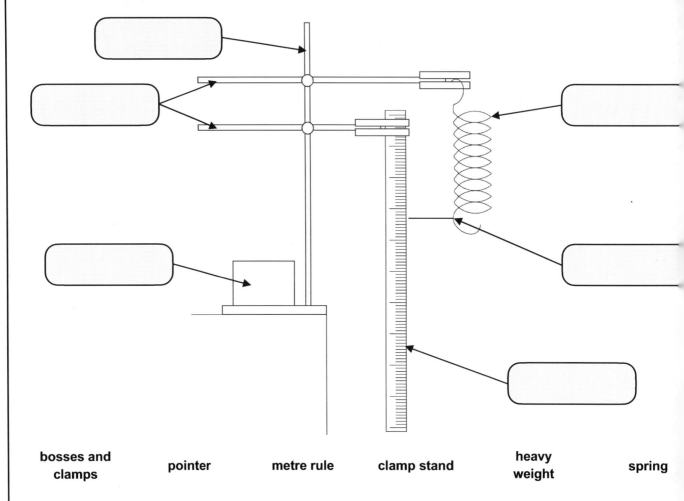

| bosses and clamps | pointer | metre rule | clamp stand | heavy weight | spring |

b. How does the heavy weight make the practical safer?

c. Complete the sentences below.

> In this experiment, the metre rule must be kept _____ and the pointer
>
> must be kept _____ . This helps to make the results accurate.
>
> Accurate results are close to the _____ value.

d. We now add a 1 N weight to the spring and measure the position of the pointer on the metre rule.

Explain how we work out the extension of the spring.

The diagram shows the position of the pointer on the metre rule.

Plot the results on the graph below and draw a line of best fit.

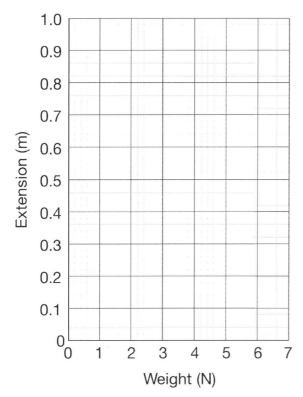

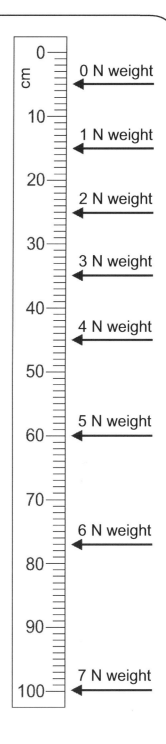

An object is hung from the same spring and produces an extension of 0.34 m.

Use the graph to determine the weight of the object.

weight = _____ N

Read the extension of the spring when a weight of 2.5 N is applied.

Use the equation on page 25 to calculate the spring constant.

The first part of the graph is linear.

What does this mean and how does this tell us that the spring is elastic?

At a certain point we overstretch the spring and exceed the limit of proportionality.

Use the graph to find the weight where we reach the limit of proportionality.

weight = _____ N

Why can we not be certain of the exact weight where we exceed the limit of proportionality?

Describe how we can change the experiment to find this weight.

Moments

1. Which of the following is the definition of a moment?

| A force causing an object to stretch | A force causing an object to compress | A force causing an object to accelerate | The turning effect of a force |

We can calculate moment using the equation below.

You are not given this equation in the exam so you need to learn it.

$$\text{Moment (Nm)} = \text{Force (N)} \times \text{Distance from pivot to line of action of force (m)}$$

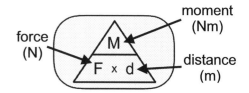

force (N) — M — moment (Nm)

F × d — distance (m)

---

2. The diagram shows a spanner being used to turn a nut.

A force of 50 N is applied.

The distance from the force to the pivot is 0.2 m.

Calculate the moment produced by the spanner.

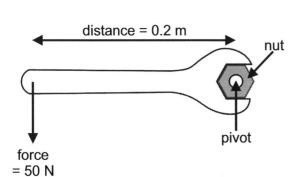

distance = 0.2 m

nut

pivot

force = 50 N

Moment = _____ N

---

3. The spanner is now used on a different nut.

The force is still 50 N.

The perpendicular distance from the force to the pivot is now 0.15 m.

a. Explain what is meant by perpendicular distance.

b. Calculate the moment produced by the spanner in this case.

Moment = _____ Nm

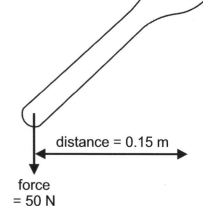

distance = 0.15 m

force = 50 N

c. Turning a nut is easier with a longer handled spanner.

Explain why.

The diagram shows a man lifting a wheelbarrow.

The man is applying a force of 100 N.

The distance from the pivot to the line of action of the force is 0.9 m.

Calculate the moment produced by the man.

Moment = _____ Nm

Describe how the wheelbarrow could be redesigned to lift the same load with a smaller force.

Explain your answer.

A moment is applied when a screwdriver is used to turn a screw.

The diagram show two different screwdrivers.

A force of 8 N is applied to the left hand screwdriver.

The distance from the pivot (the centre of the screwdriver) to the force (the edge of the handle) is 0.02 m.

Calculate the moment produced by the left hand screwdriver.

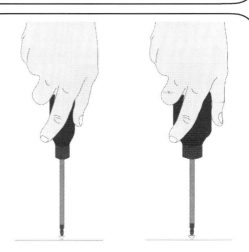

Moment = _____ Nm

Which screwdriver will require less force to turn the screw?

Explain your answer.

Balanced Moments

1. The diagram shows two people sitting on a balanced see-saw.

a. Person A has a weight of 750 N and is sitting 1.5 m from the pivot.

Calculate the anticlockwise moment.

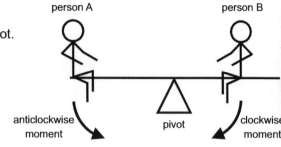

b. Which of the following statements is true?

> The clockwise moment is less than the anticlockwise moment

> The clockwise moment equals the anticlockwise moment

> The clockwise moment is greater than the anticlockwise moment

c. Explain your answer to question b.

d. Person B is sitting at a distance of 1 m from the pivot.

Calculate the weight of person B.

2. The diagram shows a crane used to lift heavy objects.

The moment of the load is counterbalanced by a counterweight.

The position of the counterweight can be changed depending on the position of the load.

a. The crane is lifting a load with a weight of 30 000 N. The distance of the load from the pivot is 8 m.

Calculate the anticlockwise moment of the load.

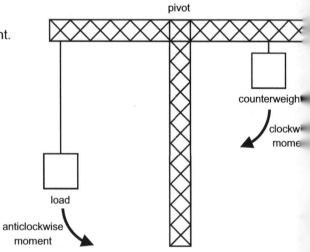

b. The counterweight has a weight of 40 000 N.

Calculate the distance of the counterweight from the pivot.

c. The crane is used to lift a load with a greater mass.

What must happen to the distance between the counterweight and the pivot? Explain your answer.

A student is balancing weights on a wooden beam.
This is shown in the diagram below.

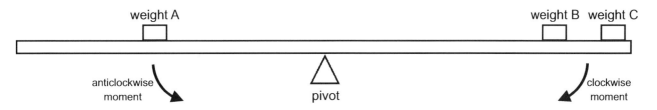

Weight A has a weight of 0.5 N and is 30 cm from the pivot.
Calculate the anticlockwise moment produced by weight A.

State the total clockwise moment produced by weights B and C together.

Weight B has a weight of 0.2 N and is 40 cm from the pivot.
Calculate the clockwise moment produced by weight B.

State the clockwise moment produced by weight C.

Weight C is 50 cm from the pivot.
Calculate the weight of weight C.

The diagram shows two identical masses.
Mass B is on a slope.
The weight due to mass A is shown by the arrow.
Draw an arrow to show the weight due to mass B.
Explain why mass A is stable but mass B will topple.
(You will need to show the pivot on mass B).

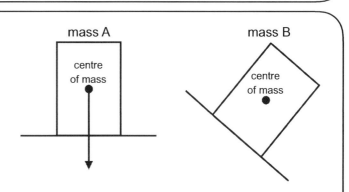

Levers and Gears

1. The diagram shows a lever being used to lift an object.

Applied
force

pivot

anticlockwise
moment

clockwise
moment

a. A force of 20 N is applied to the right hand side. This force is 1.5 m from the pivot.

Calculate the clockwise moment.

b. The clockwise moment is balanced by the anticlockwise moment from the weight of the object.

State the anticlockwise moment produced by the object.

c. The object is 0.3 m from the pivot.

Calculate the weight (ie the downward force) of the object.

d. Due to the lever, the force of the object's weight is balanced by the applied force.

A lever is a force multiplier. By how much has the applied force been multiplied?

2. A wheelbarrow is a type of lever.

Both the applied force and weight are on the same side of the pivot.

The weight of the load applies a force of 500 N at a distance of 0.4 m from the pivot.

a. Calculate the anticlockwise moment produced by this force.

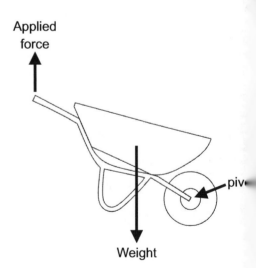

Applied
force

piv

Weight

b. State the clockwise moment produced by the applied force.

c. The applied force acts at a distance of 1.2 m from the pivot.

Calculate the applied force (to 4 significant figures).

d. By how much has the applied force been multiplied?

The diagram below shows a pair of gears.

ear A is attached to the engine and gear B is attached to the wheels of the car.

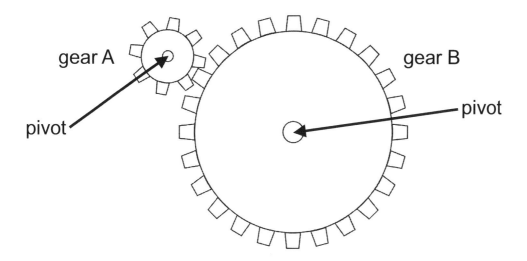

Measure the radius of gear A and gear B from the pivot to the edge of the gears.

Radius of gear A = _____ mm

Radius of gear B = _____ mm

How will gear B change the turning effect of gear A? Circle one box.

Increase x 2

Decrease x 3

Decrease x 2

Increase x 3

plain your answer.

The arrangement above is used when a car starts moving from still. This requires a very large turning effect.

₁en a car is already moving, a smaller turning effect is needed by the wheels.

this case, gear B is smaller than gear A.

plain why this would produce a smaller turning effect than the example shown above.

Explain how the work done is the same for both gear A and gear B in the above example.

Pressure in Fluids

To calculate the pressure in fluids we use the equation below.

You are not given this equation in the exam so you need to learn it.

$$\text{Pressure (Pa)} = \frac{\text{Force normal to a surface (N)}}{\text{Area of that surface (m}^2)}$$

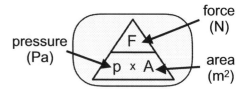

1. Gases and liquids are both examples of fluids.

The diagram shows the particles in a gas and in a liquid.

a. Describe the movement of particles in fluids.

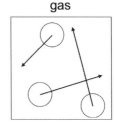

gas   liquid

b. Explain how the particles in fluids produce a pressure on the walls of the container.

c. A container is filled with gas. The surface area of the container is 5 m².

The gas exerts a force of 80 000 N on the surface of the container.

Calculate the pressure of the gas.

Pressure = _____ P

2. The atmosphere gets less dense with altitude.

The diagrams show air at the Earth's surface and at high altitude.

a. Explain why the pressure of the atmosphere is less at higher altitudes than at the Earth's surface.

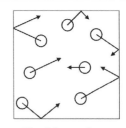 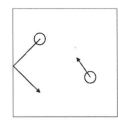

Earth's surface   High altitude

b. Explain why mountaineers take a supply of oxygen with them when they climb very tall mountains.

c. Use the idea of pressure to explain why crisp packets expand in airplanes.

Floating or Sinking

The diagram shows a tank of water with holes in the side.

Which position has the greatest pressure of water?

(position A)   (position B)   (position C)

A

Explain your answer.

B

The jet of water from C extends twice as far as the jet of water from B.

Explain why by referring to the positions of holes B and C.

C

Describe how the experiment would be different if we used a liquid with a much greater density than water.

We can calculate the pressure due to a liquid using the equation below.

You are given this equation in the exam but you are not given the units.

Pressure (Pa) = Height of column (m) x Density of the liquid (kg / m³) x gravitational field strength (N / kg)

pressure (Pa)

p

$h \times \rho \times g$

height of column (m)   density (kg / m³)   gravitational field strength (N / kg)

A diver descends in a freshwater lake to a depth of 30 m.

Calculate the pressure due to the water at this depth.

The density of fresh water is 1000 kg / m³. The gravitational field strength = 9.8 N / kg.

The diver descends to a depth of 30 m but this time in the sea.

The pressure due to the sea water at this depth was 299 880 Pa.

Calculate the density of sea water. The gravitational field strength = 9.8 N / kg.

3. The diagram shows an object in a liquid.

The diagram on the left shows how the pressure of the liquid changes with the depth of the liquid.

The diagram on the right shows the forces which are acting on the object due to the liquid.

Complete the sentences below by using the correct words from the list.

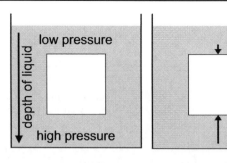

| bottom | sink | resultant | force | upthrust | depth | weight | greater |

The pressure of a liquid depends on the _____ . A greater depth has a _____

pressure. Because the _____ of an object is at a greater depth than the top, it experiences

a greater pressure. This means that the bottom of an object experiences a greater _____

than the top. Because of this, we have a _____ force acting upwards. Scientists call this

upwards force _____ . An object will float if the upthrust is equal to the _____

of the object. If the weight is greater than upthrust then the object will _____ .

---

4. The diagram shows an object before and after it is placed into a liquid.

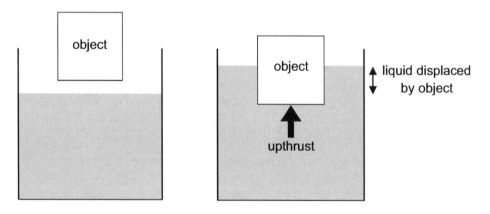

a. What can we say about the upthrust experienced by the object?

> The upthrust is less than the weight of liquid displaced by the object

> The upthrust is equal to the weight of liquid displaced by the object

> The upthrust is more than the weight of liquid displaced by the object

b. Complete the sentences below.

> An object will float if the upthrust is _____ to the weight of the object.
>
> This will happen if the object can displace its own _____ of liquid.

The diagrams shows three objects in a liquid.

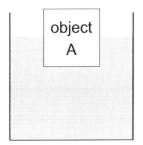 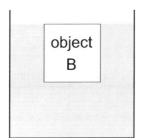 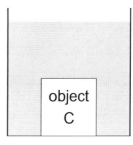

Order the objects by their weight.

Lowest weight ⟶ Greatest weight

Draw lines to connect each object to the correct statements.

Object A

Object B

Object C

This object has the same density as the liquid

This object is more dense than the liquid

This object is less dense than the liquid

Even when this object displaces its entire volume of water it still cannot displace enough water to equal its own weight

This object only has to displace a small volume of water to displace its own weight

To displace its own weight, this object must displace a volume of water equal to its own volume.

In which of the diagrams above is the weight of the object greater than upthrust?

Explain your answer.

An empty boat is floating on the sea.

Several passengers board the boat but the boat remains afloat.

Draw free body diagrams to show the forces acting on the boat when it is empty and when it contains passengers.

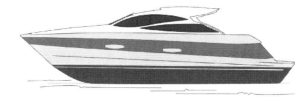

Speed

1. The diagram shows the journey taken by a cyclist.

The total distance cycled was 3100 m.

a. Show the displacement of the cyclist on the diagram.

b. Using the scale, describe the displacement in words below.

c. Explain why distance is a scalar quantity but displacement is a vector quantity.

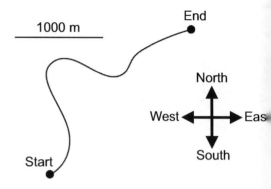

End

1000 m

North

West ← → East

South

Start

2. We carry out calculations involving speed by using the equation on the right.

You are not given this in the exam.

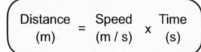

$$\text{Distance (m)} = \text{Speed (m / s)} \times \text{Time (s)}$$

distance (m)

s

v x t

speed (m / s)

time (s)

a. A person walks a distance of 750 m in 500 s.

Calculate the speed of the person.

Speed = _____ m / s

b. A person runs at a speed of 3 m / s for 1800 s.

Calculate the distance travelled by the person.

Distance = _____ m

c. A car travels a distance of 400 m in 60 s and then a further 800 m in 40 s.

Calculate the average speed of the car.

Average speed = _____ m /

3. You need to learn the typical speeds of different things.

a. Write the typical speeds of the following in the boxes below.

| walking | running | cycling | car | train | airplane | sound |

b. Describe what can affect the speed at which a person can run.

c. What happens to the speed of sound when the air is warmer? Circle one box.

| The speed of sound increases | The speed of sound decreases | The speed of sound does not change |

Velocity

We carry out calculations involving velocity by using the same equation that we saw in the previous chapter. However, unlike with speed we have to state the object's direction.

Explain why speed is a scalar quantity and velocity is a vector quantity.

Calculate the velocity of the following objects.

Object A travels a distance of 450 m in 300 s.

Object A

Distance = 450 m

North

West ← → East

South

Velocity = _____ m / s _____

Object B travels a distance of 50 m in 2 s.

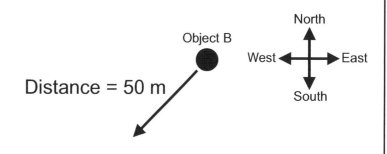

Object B

Distance = 50 m

North

West ← → East

South

Velocity = _____ m / s _____

The diagram below shows a car driving around a circular race track.

The arrow shows the direction of the car.

The speed of the car is constant.

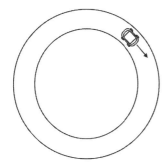
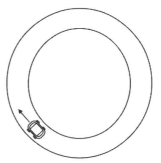

Explain how the velocity of the car is constantly changing even though the speed is constant.

Distance-Time Graphs

1. A person walked in a straight line down a street.

The journey had three parts.

Part A. The person walked a distance of 20 metres in 15 seconds.

Part B. The person stopped at a crossing for 20 seconds.

Part C. Finally the person walked a further 15 metres in 15 seconds.

a. Draw a distance-time graph for the journey.

b. Use your distance-time graph to work out the speed of the person for part A and part C.

Give your answer to 2 significant figures for part A.

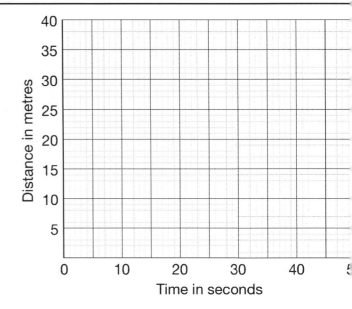

Speed during part A = _____ m / s   Speed during part C = _____ m / s

---

2. A runner was training on a straight track.

The distance-time graph is on the right.

a. Describe the runner's journey.

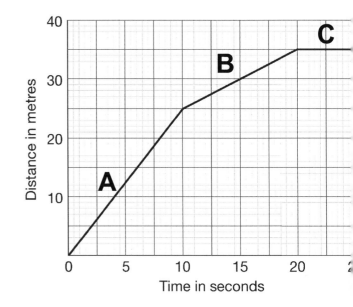

b. Calculate the speed of the runner during parts A and B.

Speed during part A = _____ m / s   Speed during part B = _____ m / s

c. How does part C show that the runner stopped?

A person is cycling down a straight road.

The distance-time graph is shown on the right.

Describe the cyclist's journey.

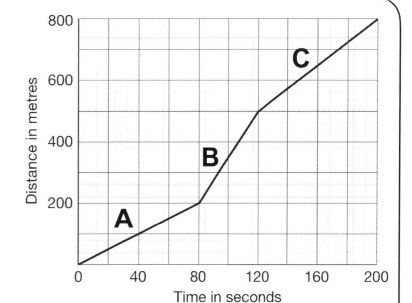

Calculate the speed of the cyclist during parts B and C.

Speed during part A =

_____ m / s

Speed during part B =

_____ m / s

Speed during part C =

_____ m / s

The distance-time graphs below show two cars driving down a straight road.

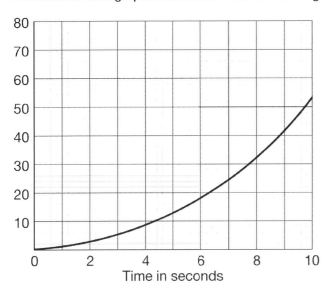

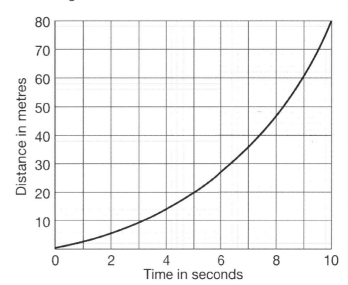

How can we tell from the distance-time graphs that the cars are accelerating?

Calculate the speed of both cars at 7 seconds.

Acceleration

To calculate the acceleration of an object we use the equation below.

You are not given this equation in the exam so you need to learn it.

$$\text{Acceleration (m / s}^2) = \frac{\text{Change in velocity (m / s)}}{\text{Time taken (s)}}$$

acceleration (m/s^2)

change in velocity (m/s)

Δv

a $\times$ t

time (s)

1. Calculate the acceleration of the following objects.

a. A train is travelling at a velocity of 40 m/s in a North West direction.

The velocity of the train increases to 50 m/s North West over a period of 10 seconds.

Acceleration = _____ m / s^2 _____

b. A cyclist is travelling North at a velocity of 4 m/s.

The velocity of the cyclist increases to 6 m/s North over a period of 8 seconds.

Acceleration = _____ m / s^2 _____

c. A person is walking South at a velocity of 1.5 m/s.

The velocity of the person increases to 2 m/s South over a period of 5 seconds.

Acceleration = _____ m / s^2 _____

d. A car is travelling at 12 m/s South East.

The car comes to a complete stop in 6 seconds.

Acceleration = _____ m / s^2 _____

2. Which of the objects above was decelerating?

Explain your answer.

A person started cycling and accelerated constantly for 30 seconds reaching a velocity of 6 m/s North. their velocity remained constant for 40 seconds. They then decelerated over 30 seconds back to a stop. Show the cyclist's journey on the velocity-time graph below.

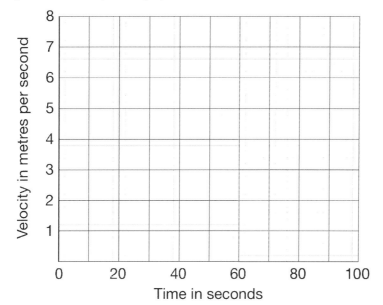

Calculate the total distance travelled by the cyclist.

The velocity-time graph below shows the journey of a car travelling East.

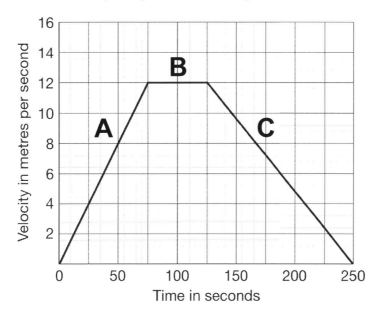

Calculate the acceleration of the car during parts A and C.

Calculate the total distance travelled by the car.

5. The velocity-time graph below shows the journey of a train travelling South.

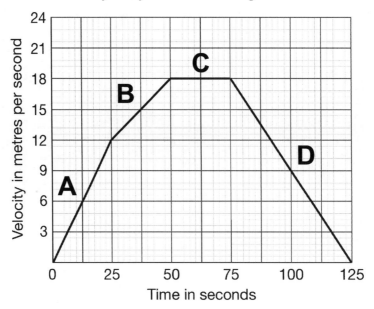

a. Calculate the acceleration of the train during parts A, B, C and D.

b. Calculate the total distance travelled by the train.

6. The velocity-time graph below shows the journey of a battery-powered toy.

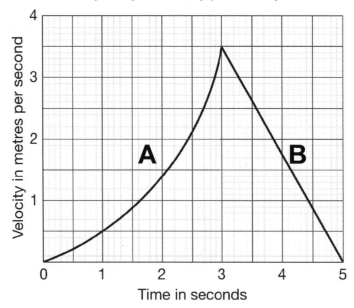

a. Explain how the graph shows a changing acceleration during A but a constant deceleration during B.

b. Calculate the total distance travelled by the toy.

Acceleration 2

To calculate the acceleration of an object we use the equation on the right.

You are given this equation in the exam.

Final velocity (m/s) → $v^2 - u^2 = 2as$ ← Distance (m)

Initial velocity (m/s)

Acceleration (m/s²)

A car is travelling at an initial velocity of 8 m/s South. It accelerates to 12 m/s South over a distance of 25 m. Calculate the acceleration of the car.

$$a = \frac{v^2 - u^2}{2s}$$

Acceleration = _____ m / s² _____

A cyclist is travelling at an initial velocity of 3 m/s West. They accelerate at 1 m/s² West over a distance of 10 m. Calculate the final velocity to 3 significant figures.

$$v^2 = 2as + u^2$$

Final velocity = _____ m / s _____

A train is travelling at an initial velocity of 10 m/s North. It accelerate at 5 m/s² North reaching a velocity of 40 m/s North. Calculate the distance the train accelerated over.

$$s = \frac{v^2 - u^2}{2a}$$

Distance = _____ m

In a previous chapter we looked at fluids. Remember that fluids are gases and liquids. Complete the sentences below by using the correct words from the list.

terminal velocity   **accelerate**   **fluid**   **resistance**   **upward**   **gravity**

A skydiver is an example of an object falling through a _____ . Initially, only the force of

_____ is acting. This causes the skydiver to _____ towards the ground at

8 m/s². However, as they fall, the skydiver experiences an _____ force due to friction

with air particles. This is called air _____ . When air resistance balances gravity, the

skydiver stops accelerating and moves at a constant velocity. This is called the _____ .

The diagram shows a free body diagram of the skydiver immediately after jumping from the airplane.

Complete the free body diagram on the right to show the forces acting on the skydiver when they reach terminal velocity.

force due to gravity ↓

Newton's First Law of Motion

1. The diagram below shows six objects. A, C and D are stationary. B, E and F are moving.

Match the objects to the correct descriptions below.

A

50 N → B ← 50 N
Velocity =
5 m/s East

50 N ↓ C 50 N ↑

25 N → D ← 25 N

25 N ↓ E 25 N ↑
Velocity =
20 m/s West

F
Velocity =
10 m/s South

Vertical forces are balanced. No horizontal forces are acting. Velocity remains constant.

Horizontal forces are balanced. No vertical forces are acting. Object remains stationary.

Vertical forces are balanced. No horizontal forces are acting. Object remains stationary.

No horizontal or vertical forces are acting. Velocity remains constant.

Horizontal forces are balanced. No vertical forces are acting. Velocity remains constant.

No horizontal or vertical forces are acting. Object remains stationary.

2. Complete the boxes below to describe Newton's First Law of Motion.

If a resultant force of zero acts on a stationary object then the object will

_____

If a resultant force of zero acts on a moving object then the object will

_____

_____

The diagram below shows a car travelling in a straight line at a constant speed.

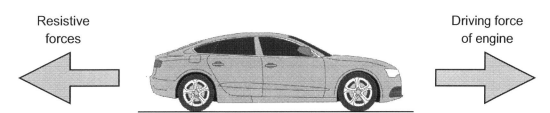

Resistive forces

Driving force of engine

How does the motion of the car tell us that the resultant force must be zero?

State the resistive forces acting on the car.

In the examples below, the resultant force acting on each object is not zero.

Each case, describe how the resultant force will affect the object and explain your answer.

Initial state of object

Effect of resultant force

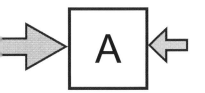

Stationary

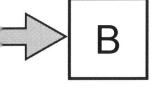

Velocity of 20 m/s
to the right

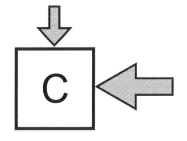

Velocity of 500 m/s
to the right

Newton's Second Law of Motion

1. Newton's Second Law of Motion is shown below.

a. Complete the sentences below by circling the correct words.

The acceleration of an object is ⟨ equal / proportional / inversely proportional ⟩ to the resultant force

and ⟨ equal / proportional / inversely proportional ⟩ to the mass of the object

b. Which of the symbols below means "proportional to"? Circle one box.

The diagram below shows the forces acting on different objects.

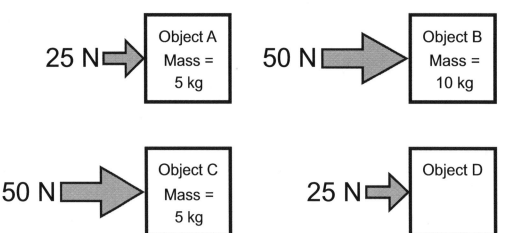

c. Explain why object C will have twice the acceleration of object A.

d. Explain why object B will have half the acceleration of object C.

e. Explain why objects A and B will have the same acceleration.

f. Object D has the same acceleration as object C.

State the mass of object D and explain your answer.

We can calculate the acceleration of an object due to a resultant force using the equation below.

ou are not given this in the exam so you need to learn it.

$$\text{Force (N)} = \text{Mass (kg)} \times \text{Acceleration (m/s}^2)$$

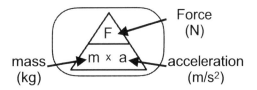

A car with a mass of 1000 kg accelerates by 3 m/s^2.

alculate the resultant force acting on the car.

Resultant force = _____ N

A cyclist and cycle have a mass of 100 kg. The cyclist applies a resultant force of 200 N.

alculate the acceleration produced.

Acceleration = _____ m/s^2

A van accelerates by 2 m/s^2. The resultant force was 6000 N.

alculate the total mass of the van and driver.

Mass = _____ kg

The symbol $\sim$ means "approximately".

mplete the boxes to show the values commonly found on UK roads.

In the UK, cars travel at speeds of $\sim$ _____ m/s on main roads and $\sim$ _____ m/s on motorways.

To accelerate from a main road to a motorway the acceleration is typically $\sim$ _____ m/s^2.

For a typical family car, this requires a force of $\sim$ _____ N.

Newton's Second Law of Motion also explains the idea of inertia.

What is meant by the word "inertia"?

In question 2c, we calculated the mass of an object from the force and the acceleration. This is the inertial mass.

w does the inertial mass affect the force needed to produce a given acceleration?

cle the correct word.

If an object has a larger inertial mass, it will require a smaller / greater force to

produce a given acceleration compared to an object with a smaller inertial mass

Newton's Third Law of Motion

1. Complete the sentence below to describe Newton's Third Law of Motion.

> Whenever two objects interact, the forces they exert on each other are _____ in magnitude but _____ in direction

2. The following diagrams represent pairs of forces in action.

In each case, draw arrows to show the forces involved.

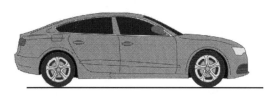

> The wheels exert a backwards force on the road. The road exerts a forward force on the wheels.

> The man exerts a pull force acting backwards on the rope. The rope exerts a pull force acting forwards on the man.

> The man uses the paddle to exert a backwards push force onto the water. The water exerts a forwards push force onto the paddle.

> The rocket exerts a downwards push force on the exhaust gases. The exhaust gases exert an upwards push force on the rocket.

S   N   S   N

> The left magnet exerts a force of attraction on the right magnet and the right magnet exerts a force of attraction on the left magnet.

> The Earth exerts a downwards force of attraction due to gravity on the skydiver and the skydiver exerts an upwards force of attraction due to gravity on the Earth.

Forces Acting on a Skydiver

The forces acting on a skydiver change as the skydiver falls to Earth.

Use the words below to complete the boxes showing how the forces change.

Draw arrows to show the forces acting.

decelerate	smaller	constant	air resistance	increases
terminal	weight	decreases	friction	balance

When the skydiver leaves the airplane, only the force of _____ is acting. The size of this force will not change. Because there is a resultant force, the velocity of the skydiver _____ as they accelerate towards the ground.

As the skydiver falls, they collide with air particles. This causes the force of _____ acting upwards. Scientists call this air resistance. Because this air resistance is much _____ than weight, the skydiver continues to accelerate towards the ground.

As the skydiver's velocity increases, the air resistance increases. When air resistance _____ the force of weight there is no resultant force. Now the skydiver moves downwards at a constant velocity. Scientists call this the _____ velocity.

The skydiver now opens their parachute. _____ now massively increases. Air resistance is now much greater than weight so there is a resultant force acting upwards. This causes the skydiver to _____ (their velocity decreases).

As the velocity decreases, the air resistance _____. At some point, air resistance and weight are balanced. Now the skydiver moves downwards at a _____ velocity. This is the new (lower) terminal velocity.

2. The graph below shows the velocity of the skydiver from when they leave the airplane.

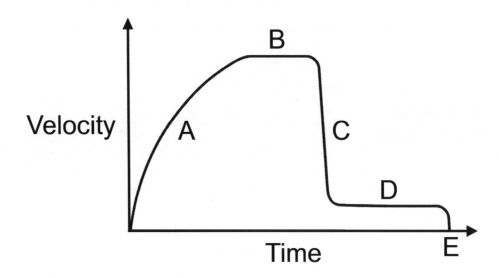

a. How can we tell from the graph that the skydiver is accelerating during part A?

b. Explain in terms of forces why the rate of acceleration decreases during part A.

c. The skydiver achieves terminal velocity during part B.

Explain what is meant by terminal velocity and explain why the skydiver could not safely land during this period.

d. The skydiver opens their parachute at the start of part C.

Explain in terms of forces why the skydiver decelerates during part C.

e. The skydiver reaches a second terminal velocity during part D.

What can we say about the forces acting during this period?

f. Why is it safe for the skydiver to land during this period of terminal velocity?

Required Practical: Acceleration

In this experiment, we investigate the factors affecting the acceleration of an object.

Label the diagram below to show the equipment needed for this practical.

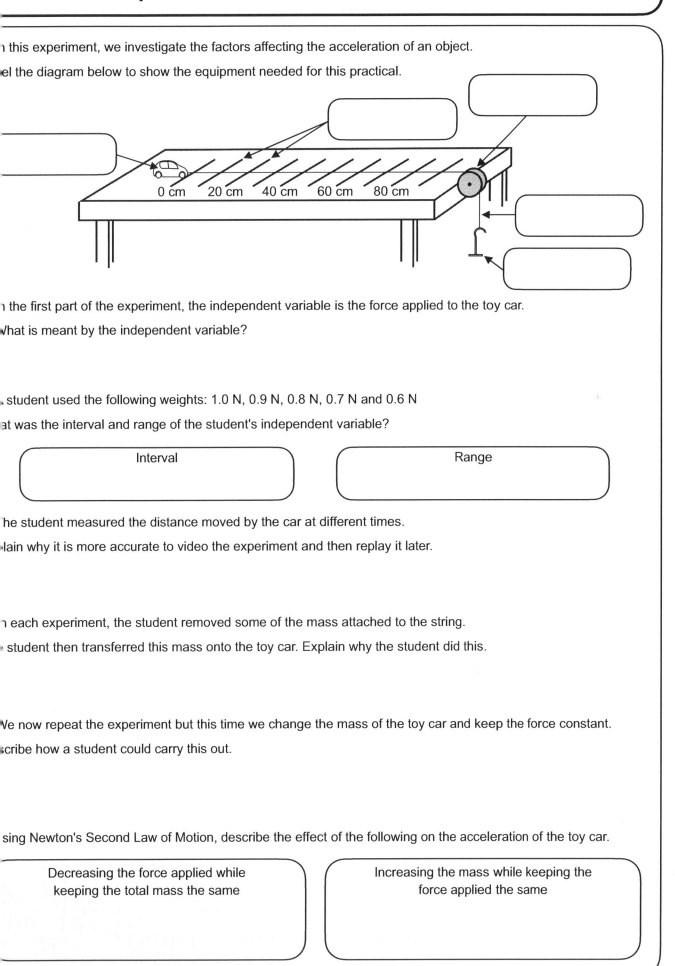

In the first part of the experiment, the independent variable is the force applied to the toy car.

What is meant by the independent variable?

A student used the following weights: 1.0 N, 0.9 N, 0.8 N, 0.7 N and 0.6 N

What was the interval and range of the student's independent variable?

Interval	Range

The student measured the distance moved by the car at different times.

Explain why it is more accurate to video the experiment and then replay it later.

In each experiment, the student removed some of the mass attached to the string.

The student then transferred this mass onto the toy car. Explain why the student did this.

We now repeat the experiment but this time we change the mass of the toy car and keep the force constant.

Describe how a student could carry this out.

Using Newton's Second Law of Motion, describe the effect of the following on the acceleration of the toy car.

Decreasing the force applied while keeping the total mass the same	Increasing the mass while keeping the force applied the same

Vehicle Stopping Distance

1. One of the most important aspects of driving a car is the time taken for the car to stop in an emergency.

This involves the thinking distance, the braking distance and the stopping distance.

Write the definitions of these in the boxes below.

> Thinking Distance

> Braking Distance

> Stopping Distance

2. The diagram below shows how the stopping distance of a car varies with the speed of the car.

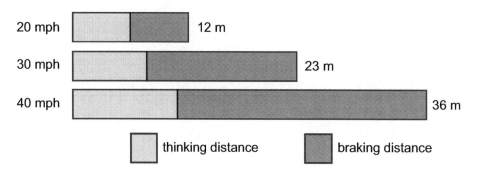

20 mph	12 m
30 mph	23 m
40 mph	36 m

thinking distance   braking distance

a. These stopping distances are for cars under ideal conditions.

Suggest what is meant by ideal conditions.

b. 30 miles per hour is a common speed limit on UK main roads.

On many residential streets, the speed limit is reduced to 20 miles per hour.

Suggest why the speed limit is often reduced on residential streets.

c. At 30 mph the stopping distance is at least six car lengths.

Explain why it is dangerous to drive too closely to the car in front.

We can measure a person's reaction time by using a ruler.

Describe how a ruler can be used to measure a person's reaction time.

Energy drinks contain caffeine which is a stimulant.

Two students measured their reaction times before and after drinking an energy drink.

The results are shown in the table below.

Student	Reaction time in seconds before energy drink			Mean	Reaction time in seconds after energy drink			Mean
	Repeat 1	Repeat 2	Repeat 3		Repeat 1	Repeat 2	Repeat 3	
A	0.80	0.65	0.80	0.75	0.40	0.35	0.30	0.35
B	0.45	0.35	0.90		0.40	0.35	0.45	0.40

Describe the effect of the energy drink on person A.

Calculate the mean value for person B before the energy drink and write this in the table.

Person B had drunk a large coffee one hour before the experiment.

Explain how this is shown by the results for person B.

Many factors can increase the stopping distance for a vehicle.

Draw lines to show whether the following factors increase the thinking distance or the braking distance.

Consuming alcohol   Wet conditions   Worn tyres   Using mobile phone

Thinking Distance   Braking Distance

Icy conditions   Tired driver   Worn brakes   Using certain drugs

Force and Braking

1. Moving vehicles have a great deal of kinetic energy.

We calculate kinetic energy using the equation on the right.

a. A car with a mass of 1000 kg is moving with a velocity of 15 m / s West.

Calculate the kinetic energy of the car.

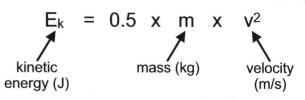

$$E_k = 0.5 \text{ x } m \text{ x } v^2$$

kinetic energy (J)   mass (kg)   velocity (m/s)

velocity = 15 m/s

b. The velocity of the car now doubles to 30 m / s West.

Calculate the kinetic energy of the car at this velocity.

c. What will happen to the kinetic energy of a car if its velocity increases by 3x?

Explain your answer.

---

2. Complete the sentences below by using the correct words from the list.

| greater | control | friction | overheat | thermal | kinetic |

When a car brakes, the brake presses against the wheel. This causes the force of _____

to act. The _____ energy store is transferred to the _____ energy store

and the temperature of the brakes increases as the car slows. If we increase the speed of the car then

_____ braking force is needed to stop the car in a given distance. Braking while at high spe

can cause the brakes to _____ or the driver to lose _____ of the vehicle.

---

3. We can calculate the forces acting on a car when it decelerates.

a. A car has a mass of 1500 kg and is travelling at a velocity of 15 m / s East.

Its velocity decreases to zero in 5 seconds. Calculate the force required.

$$\text{Force (N)} = \text{Mass (kg)} \text{ x } \text{Acceleration (m/s}^2)$$

b. A car has a velocity of 20 m / s North. The velocity decreases to 10 m / s North in 2 seconds.

The force required was 5000 N. Calculate the mass of the car.

Momentum

All moving objects have momentum.

We calculate momentum using the equation below.

You are not given this equation in the exam so you need to learn it.

$$\begin{array}{ccc} \text{Momentum} \\ \text{(kg m/s)} \end{array} = \begin{array}{c} \text{Mass} \\ \text{(kg)} \end{array} \times \begin{array}{c} \text{Velocity} \\ \text{(m/s)} \end{array}$$

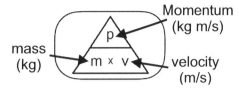

Calculate the momentum of a van with a mass of 3000 kg travelling at 20 m/s North.

Momentum = _____ kg m/s North

A moving car has a momentum of 9 600 kg m/s East. The car has a mass of 1200 kg.

Calculate the velocity of the car.

Velocity = _____ m/s East

A boy on a scooter has a velocity of 6 m/s South and a momentum of 300 kg m/s South.

Calculate the combined mass of the boy and scooter.

Mass = _____ kg

In a closed system, the total momentum before an event is equal to the total momentum after an event.

A moving car has a momentum of 10 000 kg m/s West. It collides with a stationary car and both cars move forward.

State the momentum of the stationary car.

State the total combined momentum of the cars after the collision.

Explain your answer.

The diagram shows a cannonball being ejected from a cannon.

Explain why the cannon recoils (moves backwards).

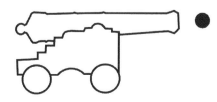

Conservation of Momentum

1. The diagram shows a skateboarder jumping off a stationary skateboard.

The skateboarder has a mass of 40 kg.

The skateboard has a mass of 4 kg.

The skateboarder jumps backwards off the skateboard with a velocity of 0.5 m/s.

a. Calculate the backwards momentum of the skateboarder.

b. State the forwards momentum of the skateboard.

c. Calculate the forwards velocity of the skateboard.

2. A van collided with a stationary car.

Both the van and car move forwards together.

The van has a mass of 3000 kg and a forwards velocity of 20 m/s. The car has a mass of 1000 kg.

Before collision

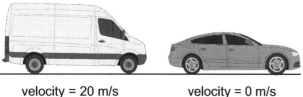

velocity = 20 m/s   velocity = 0 m/s

After collision

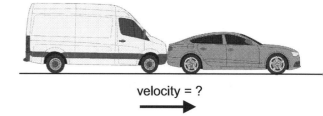

velocity = ?

a. Calculate the forward momentum of the van before the collision.

b. State the total forward momentum of the van and car after the collision.

c. Calculate the forwards velocity of the van and car together after the collision.

Change in Momentum

the momentum of an object changes, the object experiences a force.

'e can calculate the force using the equation on the right.

ɔu are given this equation so you do not need to learn it.

Force (N)	=	Mass (kg)	x	Change in velocity (m/s)
				Time (s)

The force experienced by an object depends on how rapidly the ɹange in momentum takes place.

A driver with a mass of 80 kg is travelling at 15 m/s. They lose control and crash into a wall.

ne driver is not wearing a seatbelt. The velocity of the driver falls to zero in 0.2 seconds.

ɑlculate the force experienced by the driver.

If the driver had been wearing a seatbelt, the time for the momentum change would have been 1 s.

ɑlculate the force experienced by the driver in this case.

Explain how seatbelts reduce the risk of serious injury in car crashes.

Seatbelts are designed to stretch slightly when they are engaged.

plain how this reduces the forces acting on a passenger.

ɔars also have airbags positioned in front of the driver and passengers.

ring a car crash, airbags partially fill with a gas. When a person collides with the bag, the bag slowly deflates.

ɔlain how airbags reduce the risk of serious injury.

2. A cyclist was travelling with a velocity of 6 m/s. The cyclist loses control and their head collides with the paveme

The cyclist was wearing a bike helmet. The velocity of the cyclist decreased to zero in 0.5 s.

a. Calculate the force experienced by the cyclist's head (the mass of the cyclist's head was 5 kg).

b. If the cyclist had not been wearing a bike helmet, their velocity would have decreased to zero in 0.1 s.

Calculate the force experienced by the cyclist's head in this case.

c. Cycle helmets are not rigid. They contain expanded polystyrene which can be crushed.

Explain the benefit of this design compared to a rigid helmet.

3. During a high jump, athletes jump over a horizontal pole before landing on a crash mat.

A high jumper has a mass of 70 kg. When they land on the crash mat, they experience a force of 700 N.

The high jumper takes 0.5 s to stop.

Calculate the velocity of the high jumper as they first land on the mat.

4. Children's playgrounds usually have a soft surface, often made of rubber.

A child fell from a climbing frame onto the surface, experiencing a force of 600 N.

The velocity of the child decreased from 4 m/s to zero in 0.25 s.

Calculate the mass of the child.

Chapter 2 : Waves

- Describe the differences between transverse and longitudinal waves and give examples of these types of waves.

- Describe what is meant by the wavelength, amplitude, frequency and time period of a wave and label these on a wave diagram (where appropriate).

- Use the wave equation to calculate wave speed, frequency or wavelength of a wave.

- Describe how to measure the speed of sound in air.

- Describe how to measure the properties of water waves using a ripple tank (required practical).

- Describe how to measure the properties of waves in a solid (required practical).

- Describe how waves are reflected and draw a ray diagram to show the position of the image produced by reflected light rays.

- Describe how to investigate the reflection and refraction of light waves (required practical).

- Describe the features of sound waves and explain how sound waves can change from one medium to another.

- Relate the frequency and amplitude of sound waves to the features of the sound.

- Describe what is meant by ultrasound and explain how ultrasound can be used to visualise internal organs and determine the distance to objects.

- Describe the features and properties of P waves and S waves and how these have been used to determine the internal structure of the Earth.

- Describe the features of electromagnetic waves and place the EM waves in order of frequency / wavelength.

- Describe how waves can be refracted when they change speed and explain this using the idea of wavefronts.

- Describe how to investigate the emission and absorption of infrared radiation (required practical).

- Describe what happens when EM radiation is emitted or absorbed by atoms.

- Describe the hazards of EM radiation.

- Describe how radio waves are emitted and what happens when radio waves are absorbed.

Chapter 2 : Waves

- Describe the uses of the different waves of the electromagnetic spectrum.

- Describe what is meant by a convex lens and draw ray diagrams to show the position and nature of the image produced by a convex lens.

- Describe how a convex lens can be used as a magnifying glass and calculate the magnification produced by a convex lens.

- Describe what is meant by a concave lens and draw ray diagrams to show the position and nature of the image produced by a concave lens.

- Describe the difference between specular and diffuse reflection.

- Describe how different filters and surfaces lead to different colours of visible light.

- Describe what is meant by black body radiation.

- Describe how the temperature of an object can be affected by the amount of radiation absorbed or emitted by the object.

- Describe the effect of the atmosphere on radiation emitted by the Sun and radiation emitted by the surface of the Earth.

Transverse and Longitudinal Waves

Waves are either transverse or longitudinal.

All waves transfer energy from one place to another.

Complete the boxes below to show the features of water waves and sound waves in air.

> **Water waves**
>
> Type of wave: transverse / longitudinal
>
> Energy transferred = _____

> **Sound waves in air**
>
> Type of wave: transverse / longitudinal
>
> Energy transferred = _____

The diagram below shows a transverse wave.

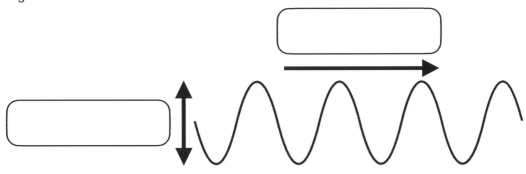

Label the diagram to show the oscillations and the direction of energy transfer.

All of the following statements are false.

Write the correct versions in the spaces on the right.

The movement of the transverse wave sideways is called an oscillation →	
In transverse waves, the oscillations are parallel to the direction of energy transfer →	
In the transverse wave above, the direction of energy transfer is up and down →	
Water waves are a longitudinal wave →	

Complete the sentences below describing the key feature of transverse waves.

In transverse waves, the oscillations are _____ to the direction of energy transfer.

Perpendicular means at _____ angles.

3. The diagram below shows a sound wave travelling through air.

The diagram also shows the air particles.

Sound waves in air are longitudinal.

a. Label the diagram to show the oscillations and the direction of energy transfer.

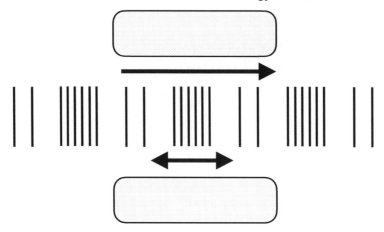

b. The diagram below shows the air particles which the sound waves are travelling through.

Label the compressions and rarefactions on the diagram.

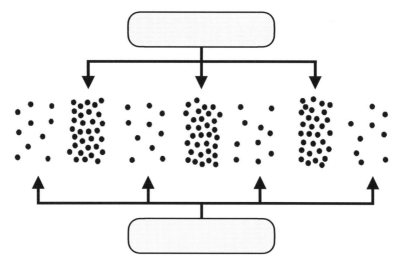

c. Complete the sentences below by selecting the correct words from the boxes.

In a compression, the particles are   closer together / further apart

In a rarefaction, the particles are   closer together / further apart

d. In a longitudinal wave, what can we say about the direction of oscillation and direction of energy transfer?

e. Describe another difference between longitudinal waves and transverse waves.

Exam tip: Remember that in both water waves and sound waves in air,
it is the wave that travels and not the water or the air

Properties of Waves

The amplitude is an important property of waves.

Complete the sentences below by using the correct words from the list.

displacement   **vibrates**   **amplitude**   **undisturbed**

_____ of a wave is the maximum _____ of a point on a wave from

_____ position, in other words the furthest point the wave _____ .

diagrams below show two waves.

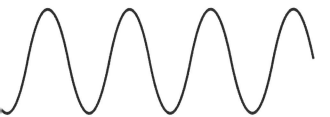

Circle the correct box to show the type of wave in both cases.

(Longitudinal)   (Transverse)

On the diagrams, label the undisturbed position and the amplitude.

---

another important property of waves is the wavelength.

Which of the boxes below shows the correct definition of the wavelength?

The time in seconds for one wave to pass a point	The number of waves passing a point each second
The distance from a point on one wave to the equivalent point on the adjacent wave	The maximum displacement of a point on a wave from its undisturbed position

Use a ruler to measure the wavelength in mm of the following transverse waves.

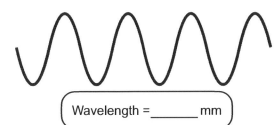

Wavelength = _____ mm

Wavelength = _____ mm

Wavelength = _____ mm

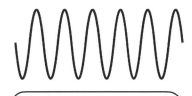

Wavelength = _____ mm

3. Measuring the wavelength of a longitudinal wave is more tricky.

To do this, measure the distance from the centre of one compression to the next or one rarefaction to the next.

a. Measure the wavelength of the two longitudinal waves below.

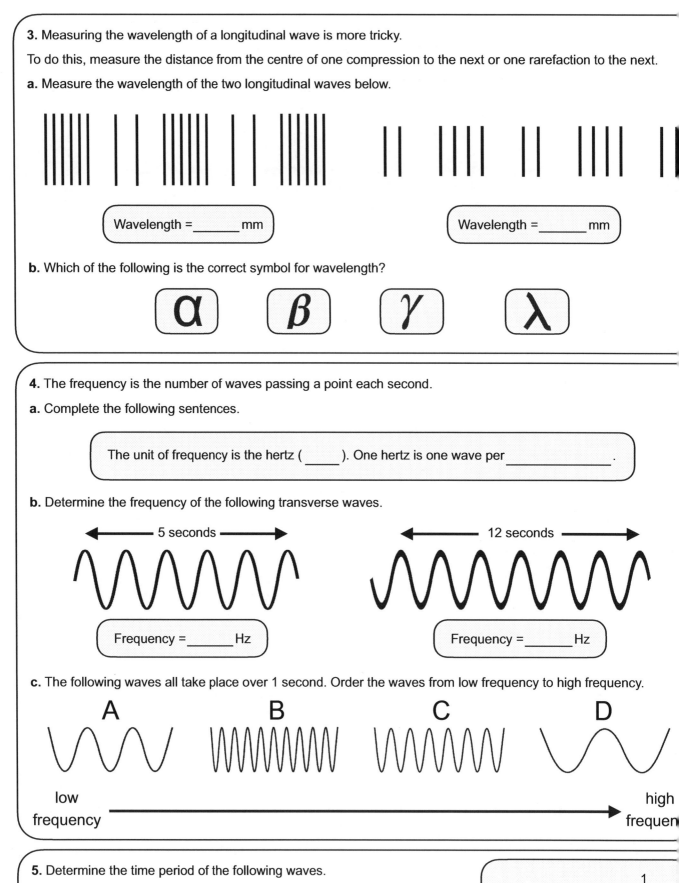

Wavelength =_____ mm

Wavelength =_____ mm

b. Which of the following is the correct symbol for wavelength?

α   β   γ   λ

4. The frequency is the number of waves passing a point each second.

a. Complete the following sentences.

The unit of frequency is the hertz (_____). One hertz is one wave per _____ .

b. Determine the frequency of the following transverse waves.

◄——— 5 seconds ———►

◄——— 12 seconds ———►

Frequency =_____ Hz

Frequency =_____ Hz

c. The following waves all take place over 1 second. Order the waves from low frequency to high frequency.

A   B   C   D

low
frequency

high
frequen

5. Determine the time period of the following waves.

Use the equation on the right. You are given this in the exam.

$$\text{Time period (s)} = \frac{1}{\text{frequency (H}}$$

a. A wave has a frequency of 20 Hz.

b. A wave has a frequency of 0.5 Hz.

The Wave Equation

You are not given the wave equation in the exam so you need to learn it.

Wave speed
(m / s)
=
Frequency
(Hz)
x
Wavelength
(m)

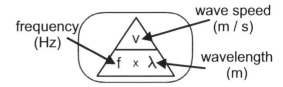

Remember to check that the units are correct when using the wave equation.

A wave has a frequency of 50 Hz and a wavelength of 3 m.

Calculate the speed of the wave.

A microwave has a frequency of 600 megahertz and a wavelength of 0.5 m.

Calculate the speed of the wave. (The prefix "mega" means "one million").

A water wave has a frequency of 20 Hz and a wavelength of 5 cm.

Calculate the speed of the wave.

You will need to rearrange the wave equation to answer the following questions.

A sound wave has a speed of 330 m/s and a frequency of 400 Hz.

Calculate the wavelength of the sound wave.

Seismic waves are caused by earthquakes.

A seismic wave had a speed of 6 km / s and a wavelength of 2 km.

Calculate the frequency of the seismic wave.

3. A method for measuring the speed of sound in air is shown below.

- Person A holds a pair of cymbals and person B holds a timer.
- Person A and B move 500 m apart.
- Person B starts timing when they see person A crash the cymbals together.
- Person B stops timing when they hear the sound of the cymbals.
- To calculate the speed of the sound waves, we divide the distance between persons A and B by the time taken.

a. There are two main sources of inaccuracy in this method.

These are shown below.

For each source of inaccuracy, explain the effect of the problem and suggest a method to reduce the problem.

	Every person has a different reaction time	The time interval between seeing the cymbals clash and hearing the sound is very short
Effect of the problem		
How to reduce the problem		

The table below shows the results of this experiment.

Person	A	B	C	D	E	F	G	H	I	J	K
Time taken in seconds between seeing cymbals clash and hearing sound	1.32	1.74	1.69	1.47	1.53	1.41	1.37	1.65	2.78	1.56	1.43

b. Which of the results do you think is anomalous?

Suggest a reason for this result.

c. Calculate the mean value for the time taken between seeing the cymbals clash and hearing the sound.

Give your answer to 3 significant figures.

d. Use your answer to question 3c to calculate the speed of sound in air from this experiment.

Give your answer to the nearest whole number.

Required Practical: Ripple Tank

ripple tank allows us to look at the features of water waves.

diagram shows a ripple tank. Label the diagram using the labels below.

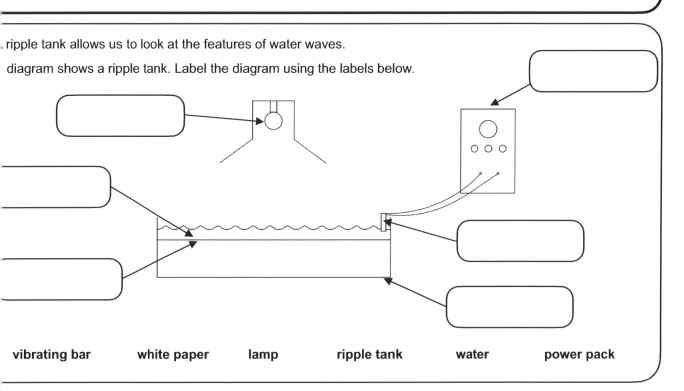

vibrating bar **white paper** **lamp** **ripple tank** **water** **power pack**

Ve can use the ripple tank to measure the wavelength.

rst we place a ruler on the paper. We then record the waves using a mobile phone and freeze the image.

Ve then measure the distance between the first wave and then ten waves further.

o find one wavelength, we divide the total length by 10.

a ruler to measure the wavelength of the waves in the examples below.

Wavelength = _____

Wavelength = _____

3. We can also use the ripple tank to measure the frequency of the waves.

a. Complete the sentences by inserting the correct words into the spaces.

The frequency is the number of waves passing a point each _____

The unit of frequency is the _____ (Hz).

The method for measuring the frequency of the water waves is shown below.

- First we place a timer next to the paper.
- We then count the number of waves passing a point in ten seconds.
- To find the frequency, we divide the total number of waves by 10.

b. The diagrams below show the same ripple tank ten seconds apart.

Use the diagram to work out the frequency of the waves.

| 00:00 | | 10:00 |

Frequency = _____ Hz

4. If we know the frequency and the wavelength, we can use the wave equation to calculate the speed of the wav

a. A wave has a frequency of 5 Hz and a wavelength of 0.06 m.

Calculate the speed of the waves.

b. Describe another way to determine the speed of waves on a ripple tank.

Required Practical: Waves in a Solid

To investigate waves in a solid, we use the following apparatus.

Label the diagram using the labels below.

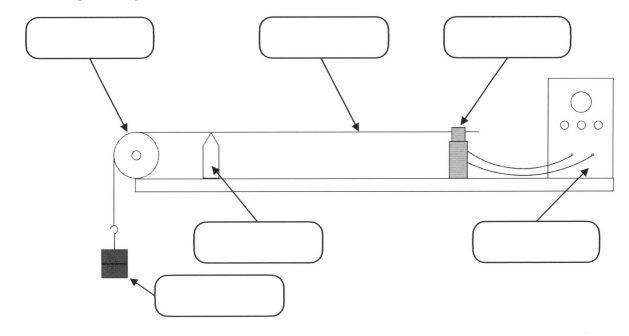

string   **vibration generator**   **signal generator**   **wooden bridge**   **mass**   **pulley**

Describe the purpose of the mass and the signal generator.

mass

signal generator

If we increase the frequency, we get a wave like the one shown below.

This is called a standing wave and is due to an effect called resonance.

In which type of musical instruments do we find standing waves like this?

Measure the wavelength (in metres) of the wave in the diagram above.

This wave was produced by a frequency of 20 Hz.

Use the wave equation on the right to calculate the speed of the wave.

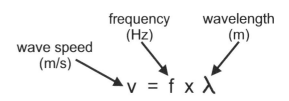

frequency (Hz)   wavelength (m)

wave speed (m/s)

$$v = f \times \lambda$$

2. If we change the frequency, we can change the shape of the standing wave.

The diagram shows the standing wave in the same piece of string as in question 1 but with a frequency of 30 Hz.

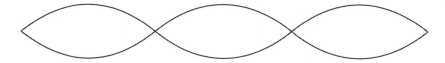

a. How many half-wavelengths are on this standing wave?

To determine the wavelength, we measure the total length of the entire standing wave.

We then divide this by the number of half-wavelengths to find the length of one half-wavelength.

Finally, we multiply by two to find the length of one complete wavelength.

b. Determine the wavelength of the wave above.

c. The wave above had a frequency of 30 Hz.

Use the wave equation to determine the speed of the wave.

d. All of the standing waves below were generated on the same string as the waves above.

In each case, determine the wavelength and the speed of each wave. The frequency is given.

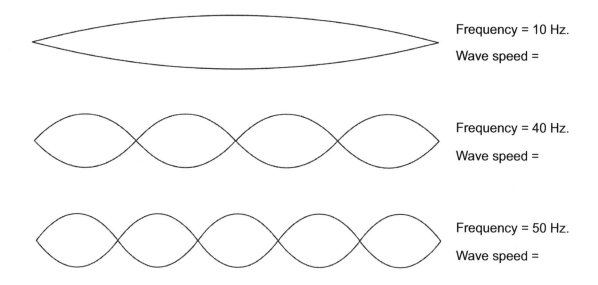

Frequency = 10 Hz.

Wave speed =

Frequency = 40 Hz.

Wave speed =

Frequency = 50 Hz.

Wave speed =

e. Which of the following factors affects the speed of a wave in a piece of string?

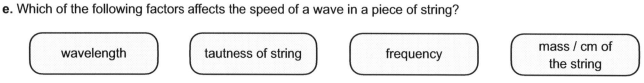

| wavelength | tautness of string | frequency | mass / cm of the string |

f. Describe how a student could change the tautness of the string.

g. Apart from changing the frequency, how could we change the equipment to adjust the standing wave on the stri

Reflection of Waves

. The diagram shows three waves hitting a boundary with a different material eg a glass block.
he arrows show the direction of the waves.

. Label the diagram using the labels below.

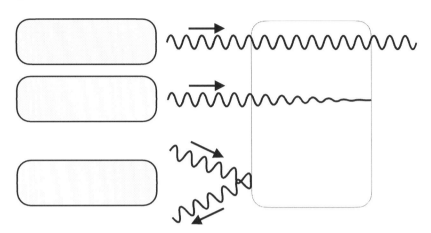

**wave is reflected off
material surface**　　　　**wave is transmitted
through material**　　　　**energy of wave is
absorbed by material**

. Complete the sentences below by using the correct words from the list.

refraction　　transmitted　　boundary　　reflected　　wavelength　　absorbed　　direction

hen a wave hits a _____ with a different material, three things can happen to the wave.

1e wave can be _____ through the material. In this case neither the wavelength nor

e_____ of the wave have changed (however, in certain cases the wave can change

rection - this is called _____). In some cases, the energy of the wave can be

_____ . If this happens then the wave may not pass through the material at all. The wave

uld simply be _____ off the surface of the material. Which of these happens depends

the _____ of the wave.

The diagram shows a light ray reflecting off the surface of
mirror.

bel the diagram to show the following:

mirror　　**incident
ray**　　**reflected
ray**　　**normal**

**angle of
incidence**　　**angle of
reflection**

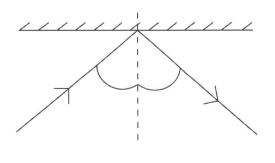

3. By drawing a ray diagram, we can work out the position of a reflection in a mirror.

a. Complete the sentence below by deleting the incorrect words.

The angle of reflection is less than / greater than / equal to the angle of incidence

b. The diagram below shows objects in front of two mirrors.

The incident and reflected rays have been drawn for you.

Complete the ray diagrams to show the position of the images in the mirrors.

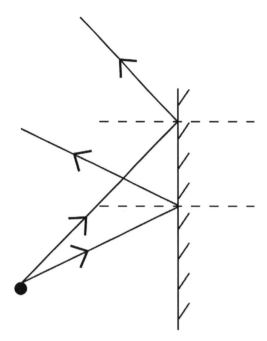
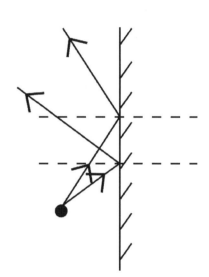

c. The diagram below shows objects in front of two mirrors.

Draw ray diagrams to show the position of the images in the mirrors.

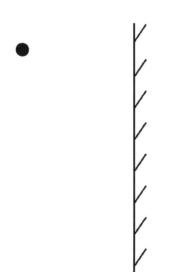

In this practical, we will use a raybox, a lens and a slit.

What is the benefit of using this equipment rather than a bulb?

Describe the main safety issue when using this set up and how can address this issue.

A3 paper

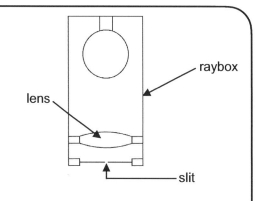

c. Next we draw a straight line down a piece of A3 paper.

We then draw another line at right angles to the first.

What piece of equipment should we use to do this?

d. What name do scientists give to the right angle line?

Label this on the diagram.

Next we place a glass block on the paper so it lies near the centre of the two lines and draw around the block.

this point we turn all the lights off in the room.

Explain why we need to turn the lights off.

ally we use the raybox to direct a ray of light towards the ss block.

e ray of light should hit the block at the normal.

What name do scientists give to this ray?

el this ray on the diagram.

What do we call the angle between this ray and the mal?

el this on the diagram.

glass block

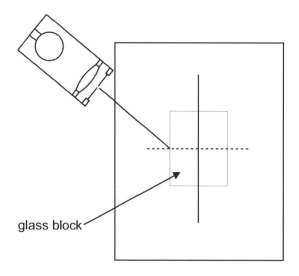

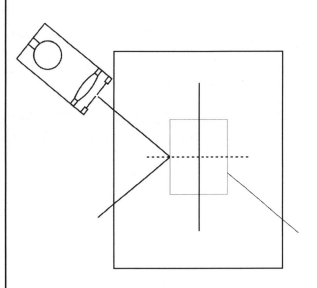

2. At this point we need to adjust the position of the ray box.

At a certain angle of incidence, we will see a ray reflect from the surface of the glass block.

a. What name do scientists give to this ray?

Label this ray on the diagram.

b. We will also see another ray leaving the block from the opposite side.

This is the transmitted ray.

Label this ray on the diagram.

c. Now we draw crosses to mark the paths of the incident ray, the reflected ray and the transmitted ray.

We also turn on the room lights.

Draw lines to show the path of the incident ray, the reflected ray and the transmitted ray.

d. We also draw a line to show the path of the transmitted ray through the block.

Draw the path of this ray on the diagram (remember to include arrows showing the direction of the ray).

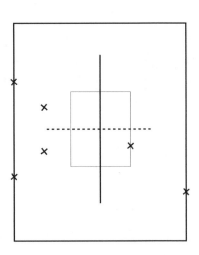

e. Now we use a protractor to measure the angle of incidence, the angle of reflection and the angle of refraction.

Label these angles on the diagram and write the values below.

Angle of incidence =	Angle of reflection =	Angle of refraction =

f. What can we say about the angle of reflection compared to the angle of incidence?

g. Finally we repeat the experiment using a block made of a different material for example a plastic such as Perspex.

How would we expect the angle of incidence, angle of reflection and angle of refraction to compare between the glass block and the Perspex block?

Explain your answer.

Sound Waves

. Sound travels when sound waves move from one place to another.

. Which of the following is true? Circle the correct box.

> Sound waves are always transverse waves

> Loud sounds are transverse waves but quiet sounds are longitudinal waves

> Sound waves in air are always longitudinal waves

. What happens to the air particles when sound waves travel through air?

The diagrams below show a microphone and the human ear.

xplain how sound waves pass from one medium to another in these examples.

Microphone

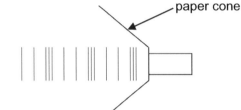
paper cone

Human Ear

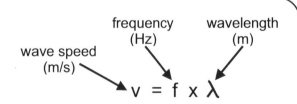
ear drum

Explain why human hearing has a frequency range of between 20 Hz and 20 000 Hz.

When sound waves pass from air into a solid, the speed of e waves increases.

Explain in terms of particles why the speed of sound in a lid is greater than the speed of sound in air.

frequency (Hz)   wavelength (m)

wave speed (m/s)

$$v = f \times \lambda$$

Explain why the frequency does not change when sound waves pass from air into a solid.

When the speed of sound increases, the wavelength also increases.

e the wave equation above to explain why this happens.

3. Sound waves cannot be viewed directly.

However, if we connect a microphone to a cathode ray oscilloscope, we get an idea of the features of sound wave

a. What is the main problem with representing sound waves using a cathode ray oscilloscope?

The diagram below shows four sound waves shown on a cathode ray oscilloscope.

Assume that the time shown across the screen is the same for each diagram.

 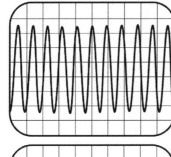 

 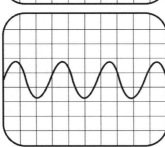 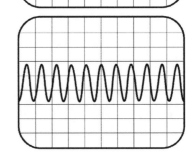

b. Draw lines to connect the description of the sound to the correct trace above.

| Trace A | Trace B | Trace C | Trace D |

| This is a relatively quiet sound with a high pitch | This is a relatively loud sound with a high pitch | This is a relatively quiet sound with a low pitch | This is a relatively lou sound with a low pitc |

c. Complete the sentences below by selecting the correct words.

Louder sounds have a greater amplitude / frequency than quieter sounds.

Higher pitched sounds have a greater amplitude / frequency than lower pitched sounds.

4. Unlike light waves, sound waves need a medium to travel through.

a. Explain why sound waves need a medium to travel through and cannot travel through a vacuum.

b. What do we call a reflected sound wave?

Ultrasound

Ultrasound has many applications in medicine and in industry.

Which of the following shows the frequency of ultrasound?

Less than 20 Hz	20 Hz to 20 000 Hz	Greater than 20 000 Hz

Explain why humans cannot hear ultrasound.

The diagram shows ultrasound waves reflecting off a kidney.

What does this tell us about the densities of the kidney and the surrounding tissue?

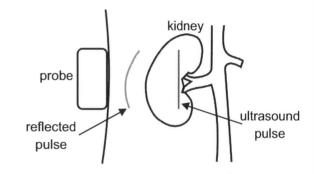

Explain why using ultrasound is safer than using X rays to view internal organs.

Suggest why ultrasound cannot be used to view the brain.

Describe how ultrasound can be used in industry.

Ultrasound can be used to determine distance.

To do this, we use the equation on the right.

$$\text{Distance (m)} = \text{Speed (m/s)} \times \text{Time (s)}$$

A fishing boat used ultrasound to determine the depth of a shoal of fish.

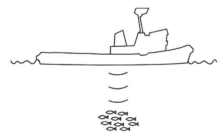

The time taken for the pulse to travel to the fish and reflect back to the ship was 0.1 s.

Determine the distance of the fish from the ship.

The speed of ultrasound in water is 1600 m/s.

b. A scientist used ultrasound to check for defects in a weld between two pieces of steel.

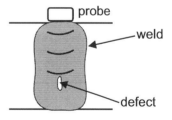

The time taken for the pulse to travel to the defect and reflect back to the probe was 1×10^{-5} s.

Determine the distance of the defect from the probe.

The speed of ultrasound in steel is 5800 m/s.

Seismic Waves

1. The diagram shows the internal structure of the Earth.

a. Complete the diagram using the correct labels and descriptions below.

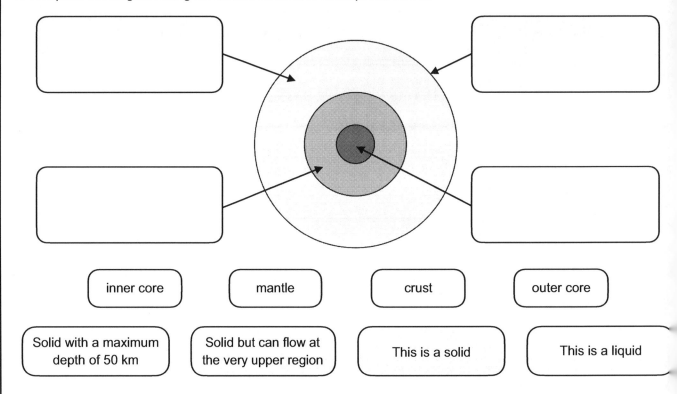

| inner core | mantle | crust | outer core |

| Solid with a maximum depth of 50 km | Solid but can flow at the very upper region | This is a solid | This is a liquid |

b. Why can scientists not directly observe the Earth's interior?

c. Complete the sentences below by using the correct words from the list.

longitudinal   **slowly**   **seismic**   **seismometers**   **tectonic**

interior   **earthquakes**   **solids**   **transverse**

Scientists have worked out the internal structure of the Earth using _____. When an

earthquake takes place, there is a sudden movement between the Earth's _____ plate

_____ waves now carry energy away from the earthquake. These waves pass throug

the Earth and are then detected by _____ in different countries. The pattern of the

seismic waves gives us information about the Earth's _____. There are two types of

seismic waves. P waves are _____ and can pass through both _____

and liquids. S waves are _____ and can only pass through solids. S waves travel

more _____ than P waves.

. The diagrams below show the patterns of S waves and P waves after an earthquake.

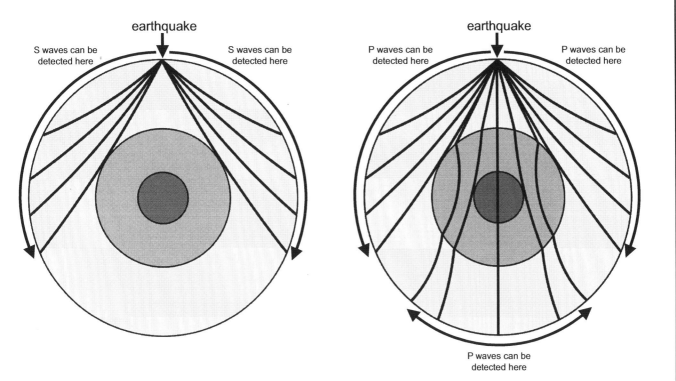

Which of the following explains why the seismic waves follow curved patterns through the Earth?

This is due to the Earth's rotation

This is due to the Earth's magnetic field

This is due to density changes in the Earth's interior

Regions where S waves cannot be detected are called the S wave shadow zone.

Label the S wave shadow zone on the diagram.

Explain why S waves do not pass into the S wave shadow zone.

Regions where P waves cannot be detected are called the P wave shadow zones.

Label the P wave shadow zones on the diagram.

Explain why P waves do not pass into the P wave shadow zones.

How did scientists work out that the Earth has a solid inner core?

Electromagnetic (EM) Waves

1. Light is just one example of a family of waves called electromagnetic (EM) waves.

a. Complete the sentences below by selecting the correct words from the boxes.

Electromagnetic waves are
> sound
> longitudinal
> transverse

waves. Like all waves, electromagnetic waves transfer energy from

one place to another. The place which generates the electromagnetic wave is called the
> origin
> source
> absorber
.

The electromagnetic waves transfer energy to the
> absorber
> origin
> source
.

b. Describe two examples of how electromagnetic waves transfer energy.

2. The spectrum of visible light is shown below.

a. Circle the correct words to show the correct frequency and wavelength.

lower / higher
frequency

shorter / longer
wavelength

| Red | Orange | Yellow | Green | Blue | Indigo | Violet |

lower / higher
frequency

shorter / long
wavelength

b. Visible light is the only part of the electromagnetic spectrum that our eyes can detect.

Complete the diagram below to show the other parts of the electromagnetic spectrum.

Circle the correct words to show the correct frequency and wavelength.

lower / higher
frequency

shorter / longer
wavelength

| | | | Visible Light | | | |

lower / higher
frequency

shorter / longer
wavelength

c. Which of the following are true statements about electromagnetic waves?

Rewrite the correct versions of the false statements in the spaces.

| EM waves form a continuous spectrum | EM waves require a medium to travel through | The speed of EM waves is 300 000 000 m/s in a vacuum | Visible light is reflected by black surfaces |

| Radio waves are the highest frequency EM waves | EM waves travel at the same speed in a vacuum | Water molecules cannot absorb the energy of microwaves | Wavelength decreases from radio waves to gamma rays |

Refraction of Waves

The diagram shows a light ray from an object passing through a glass block.

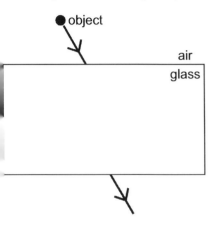

a. Draw a dashed line to show the normal where the ray enters and leaves the glass block.

b. Draw a line to connect the two parts of the ray as it passes through the block.

c. Draw the position of the image.

d. What process is taking place in the diagram?

reflection   refraction   absorption

e. Complete the sentences below to describe what is taking place in the diagram.

When the ray passes from air to glass, the speed of the wave _____ .
This causes the ray to bend _____ the normal.

When the ray passes from glass to air, the speed of the wave _____ .
This causes the ray to bend _____ the normal.

The diagrams below show rays of light passing from one medium to another.

The speed of light in medium A is greater than in medium B.

Complete the diagrams to show the path of the rays and the image.

Explain your answer in each case.

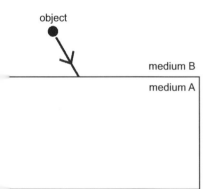

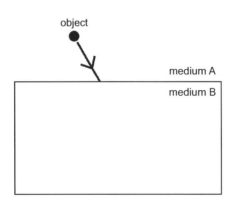

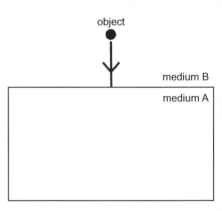

3. The diagram shows transverse waves.

All the waves have the same wavelength and the same speed.

a. Draw lines to show the wavefronts on the peaks of the waves.

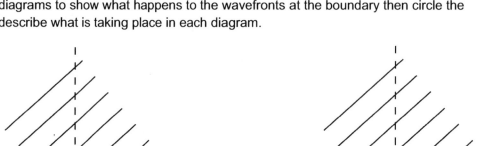

Wavefronts can be used to explain why light rays can change direction when they pass from one medium to another.

The diagram below shows light passing between different mediums.

The light waves are shown as wavefronts.

b. Complete the diagrams to show what happens to the wavefronts at the boundary then circle the correct words to describe what is taking place in each diagram.

air
glass

glass
air

When the first wavefront starts to move into the glass, those parts of the wavefront slow down / speed up.

When the first wavefront starts to move out of the glass, those parts of the wavefront slow down / speed up.

Those parts of the wavefront now get further apart / closer together.

Those parts of the wavefront now get further apart / closer together.

The wavelength of the waves increases / decreases.

The wavelength of the waves increases / decreases.

The wave changes direction away from / towards the normal.

The wave changes direction away from / towards the normal.

c. The diagram on the right shows a light wave passing from one medium to another along the normal.

Using the idea of wavefronts, explain why the direction does not change.

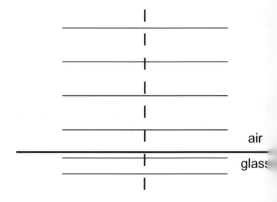

air

glass

Required Practical: Infrared

This required practical has two parts.

In the first part, we investigate how much infrared is emitted from different surfaces.

The diagram below shows the equipment that we use for this experiment.

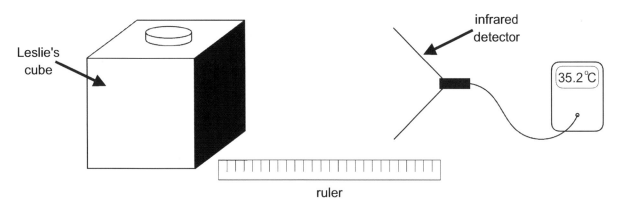

Leslie's cube has four different surfaces. These are shiny silver, shiny black, matt black and matt white.

First we fill the Leslie's cube with hot water from a kettle.

Hot water presents a danger. Describe how the following precautions could reduce the risk of injury.

| Do not use boiling water |
| Do the experiment standing up |

We now measure the temperature of the matt black surface using the infrared detector.

The variables in this experiment are listed below. Write "IV" above the independent variable, "DV" above the dependent variable and "CV" above the control variables.

| The colour of the surface pointed at the infrared detector | Distance between Leslie's cube and infrared detector | The temperature measured by the infrared detector | Temperature of the water |

The resolution is the minimum value that a measuring instrument can measure.

What is the resolution of the infrared detector shown in the above diagram?

Instead of an infrared detector, we can use a thermometer with the bulb painted black.

Explain why this may not be able to detect a difference in the amount of infrared emitted by the different surfaces.

Order the different surfaces by their emission of infrared on the arrow below.

least emission → **Emission of infrared** → greatest emission

2. In the second part of the experiment, we investigate which surfaces are best at absorbing infrared radiation.

The equipment for this experiment is shown below.

- First we use vaseline to attach a drawing pin to a sheet of metal.

- One side of the metal is painted either shiny silver, shiny black, matt black or matt white.

- We then place the sheets of metal next to an infrared heater.

- The temperature of the metal sheets increases as the surfaces absorb infrared radiation.

- We time how long it takes for the vaseline to melt and the drawing pins to fall off the metal sheets.

a. State two control variables in the experiment.

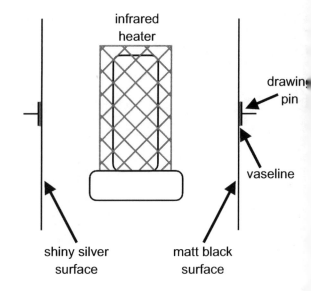

The table below shows a student's results.

	Time in seconds for drawing pin to fall off		
Colour of surface	Repeat 1	Repeat 2	Mean
Matt black	35	39	37
Shiny black	62	60	
Shiny silver	78	80	
Matt white	60	64	

b. Calculate the mean values and write these in the table (the first has been done for you).

c. Plot the results on the bar chart on the right.

d. Do the student's results show that the experiment is repeatable?

Explain your answer.

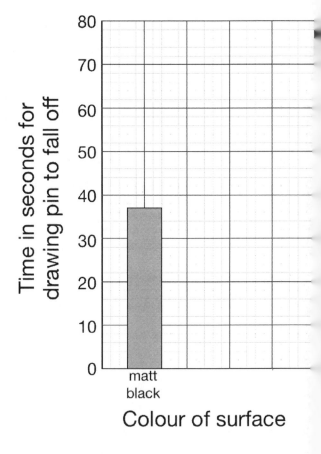

e. What do the student's results show about which surfaces are best at absorbing infrared radiation?

Properties of EM Waves 2

. The diagram below shows what happens when a lithium atom is heated.

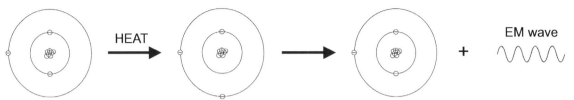

omplete the sentences below by using the correct words from the list.

electromagnetic   **energy**   **higher**   **absorb**   **visible**

When we heat an atom, _____ is absorbed. This causes an electron to move to a

_____ energy level. When the electron returns back to its original energy level,

n_____ wave is emitted. This is often in the form of _____ light.

lectrons can also change energy levels when atoms _____ electromagnetic radiation.

Electromagnetic radiation can be hazardous to the human body.

Describe the hazardous effects of ultraviolet radiation on humans.

Describe what happens when a gamma ray is emitted from an atom.

X rays and gamma rays are ionising radiation.

hich of the following best describes what is meant by ionising radiation?

Ionising radiation causes   **Ionising radiation knocks**   **Ionising radiation knocks**
atoms to form covalent bonds   **electrons off atoms**   **protons off atoms**

Explain how ionising radiation increases the risk of developing cancer.

A dental X ray has a radiation dose of 0.005 millisieverts and a chest X ray has a dose of 0.1 millisieverts.

alculate the percentage radiation dose of a dental X ray compared to a chest X ray.

The structure of atoms does not change when radio waves are emitted.

Describe how radio waves are emitted by an electrical circuit.

What happens when radio waves are absorbed by an electrical circuit?

Uses of EM Waves

Exam tip: In this section we are looking at the uses of EM waves. We look at the waves in order of low frequency to high frequency (in other words low energy to high energy).

1. Radio waves are used to transmit radio signals and terrestrial TV signals.

a. Complete the sentence below by selecting the correct word.

> Radio waves are useful for transmitting radio and TV signals because they can travel long distances without being reflected / absorbed / refracted eg by trees and buildings

b. Radio waves are reflected off a layer of the atmosphere called the ionosphere.

This allows us to send radio signals across very large distances.

This is shown in the diagram on the right.

Complete the diagram to show the reflected radio signal reaching the house.

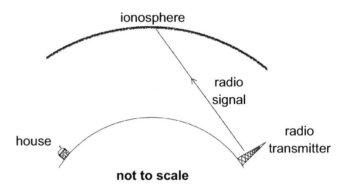

2. Microwaves have two main uses.

Microwaves can be used to communicate with satellites in space.

a. Explain why microwaves can reach satellites in space but radio waves cannot.

Microwaves are also used to heat food in microwave ovens.

b. How is the energy carried by microwaves absorbed by food?

> The energy carried by microwaves is absorbed by fat molecules

> The energy carried by microwaves is absorbed by water molecules

> The energy carried by microwaves is absorbed by protein molecules

3. The next radiation on the EM spectrum is infrared.

a. Infrared is used to heat objects. This happens in a home heating system and in normal ovens.

What type of surfaces absorb the energy of infrared radiation?

b. Explain why wrapping food in aluminium foil can prevent it burning in the oven.

c. Infrared can also be used to improve the energy efficiency of homes and offices.

Describe how we can use infrared to do this.

. Visible light is used a lot in communication.

Complete the sentences below by selecting the correct words from the boxes.

Rapid pulses of light can be sent down
| visible |
| audible |
| optical |
fibres. These are very thin strands of
| glass |
| plastic |
| metal |
.

Visible light has a short
| wavelength |
| frequency |
| amplitude |
so it can carry a lot of information eg telephone or cable TV signals.

. Ultraviolet has a range of different uses.

. Ultraviolet is used in certain types of light bulbs. The ultraviolet is converted to visible light.

Describe the advantage of these bulbs over normal light bulbs.

. Ultraviolet is also used in tanning beds. Many people think that using tanning beds is dangerous.

Describe two of the dangers of exposure to ultraviolet in tanning beds.

X rays and gamma rays are both used for imaging the internal parts of the human body.

Explain why X rays and gamma rays can be used for this whereas other parts of the EM spectrum cannot.

Describe examples where X rays and gamma rays are used in medicine.

X rays	Gamma rays

Write "T" if the following statements are true and "F" if the statements are false.

Gamma rays have a longer wavelength than X rays	Both gamma rays and X rays are examples of ionising radiation	X rays and gamma rays both increase the risk of developing cancer
Gamma rays cannot pass through the human body	Gamma rays have a higher frequency than X rays	X rays cannot pass through bones

Convex Lenses

1. The diagram on the right shows light rays pass through a convex lens.

a. Complete the sentence below.

Convex lenses are _____ at the centre than at the edges

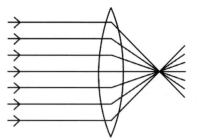

b. Label the diagram to show the principal focus and the focal length.

c. Explain why the ray passing through the centre of the lens does not change direction.

---

2. The ray diagram below shows an object placed further from the lens than twice the focal length.

a. Complete the ray diagram to show the position of the image.

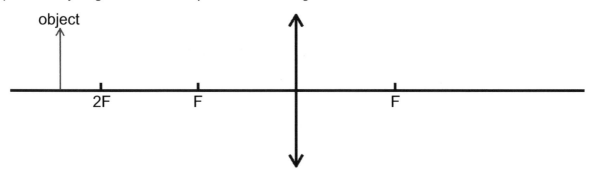

b. Tick the boxes below to show the features of the image.

| Diminished | Magnified | Inverted | Upright | Real | Virtual |

---

3. The ray diagram below shows an object placed between one and two focal lengths from the lens.

a. Complete the ray diagram to show the position of the image.

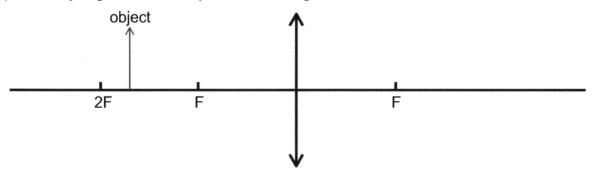

b. Describe how this image is different from the image in question 2.

---

4. If the object is at least one focal length from a convex lens then the image is always real.

Describe what is meant by a real image.

Magnifying Glasses

. Convex lenses are often used as a magnifying glass.

. What distance must the object be from the lens for it to function as a magnifying glass?

More than two focal lengths from the lens	Between one and two focal lengths from the lens	Less than one focal length from the lens

. The ray diagram below shows a convex lens acting as a magnifying glass.

omplete the ray diagram to show the position of the image.

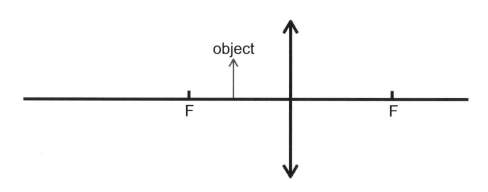

The image produced by a magnifying glass is always virtual.

escribe what is meant by a virtual image.

To calculate the magnification, we use the equation on the right.

▪is equation is given in your exam.

▪A magnifying glass is used to view an object with a height of 0.4 cm.

▪e image has a height of 3.2 cm. Determine the magnification of the lens.

$$\text{magnification} = \frac{\text{image height}}{\text{object height}}$$

▪Determine the magnification of the lens in question 1b.

▪u will need to measure the height of the image and the object.

▪A magnifying glass has a magnification of 5x. It is used to view an object with a height of 0.5 cm.

▪lculate the height of the image.

Concave Lenses

1. The diagram on the right shows light rays pass through a concave lens.

a. Complete the ray diagram to show the principal focus and the focal length.

b. Concave lenses cause light rays to diverge.

What is meant by the word "diverge"?

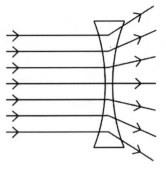

c. Explain why concave lenses produce a virtual image.

2. The two ray diagrams below show concave lenses.

a. Complete the ray diagrams to show the image produced in each case.

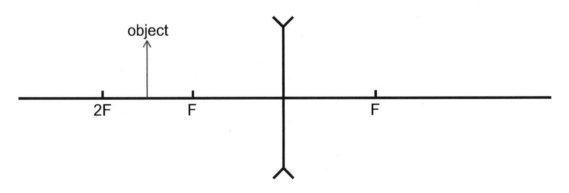

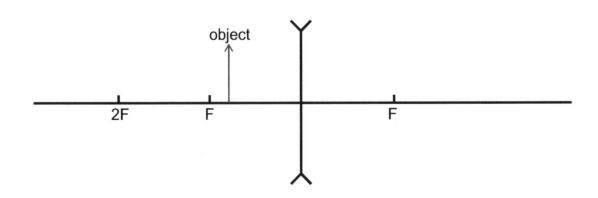

b. Which of the following are <u>always</u> the features of an image produced by a concave lens?

Tick the correct answers.

(Diminished)   (Magnified)   (Inverted)   (Upright)   (Real)   (Virtual)

Visible Light

. When light reflects, it can either show specular reflection or diffuse reflection.

raw lines between the correct boxes to show the features of these types of reflection.

| Specular reflection | This takes place on rough surfaces | All of the light rays reflect in a single direction | This produces an image | 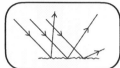 |

| Diffuse reflection | This takes place on smooth surfaces | The light rays scatter in many different directions | No image is produced | 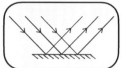 |

When we pass white light through a prism, the light splits into its different colours.

What name do scientists give to the light split into different colours?

white light

red
orange
yellow
green
blue
indigo
violet

Complete the sentence by circling the correct word.

Each colour of light has a wide / narrow band of wavelengths and frequencies

The diagrams below show several coloured filters.

hite light is shone onto one side of each filter.

hat colour will the filters appear?

xplain your answer in each case.

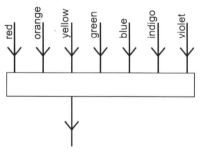

Colour of filter is: _____

Reason:

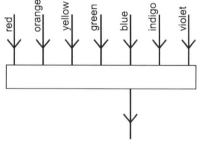

Colour of filter is: _____

Reason:

red   orange   yellow   green   blue   indigo   violet

Colour of filter is: _____

Reason:

Objects can either be transparent, translucent or opaque.

plain what is meant by transparent, translucent and opaque.

3. How light reflects can also affect the colour of an object.

a. The diagram shows white light reflecting off a white object.

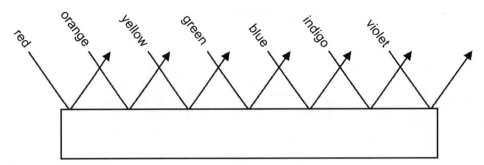

Explain why the object appears white.

b. State the colours of the objects below and explain your answer in each case.

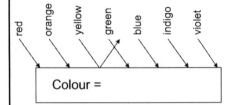

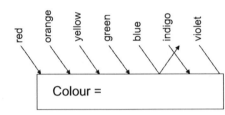

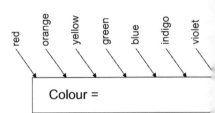

4. The diagrams show different coloured objects under different coloured filters.

a. In each case, state the colour of the object and explain your answer.

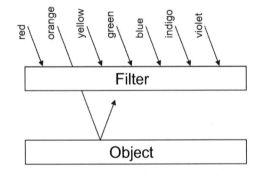

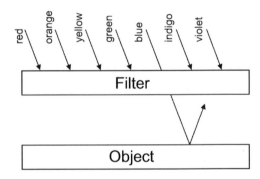

b. What colour will the object on the right appear?

Explain your answer.

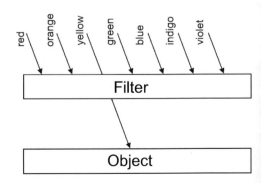

Black Body Radiation

. The amount of infrared radiation emitted and absorbed affects the temperature of an object.

. Complete the following sentences.

All objects, no matter what their temperature, both _____ and _____

infrared radiation. _____ surfaces are the best absorbers and emitters of infrared.

he graph shows the effect of temperature on the intensity and wavelength of radiation emitted from an object.

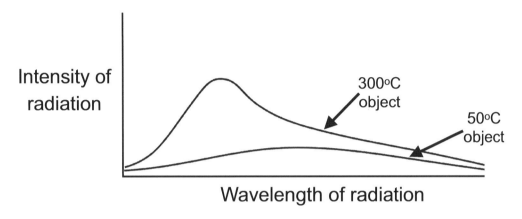

Sketch a line on the graph to represent an object at 1000°C.

As the temperature of an object increases, the intensity of radiation emitted also increases.

hat is meant by the word "intensity"?

Visible light has a shorter wavelength compared to infrared radiation.

se the graph to explain why very hot objects emit visible light.

The diagrams show two different objects absorbing
d emitting radiation.

e amplitude indicates the intensity.

Which object is a black body?

plain your answer.

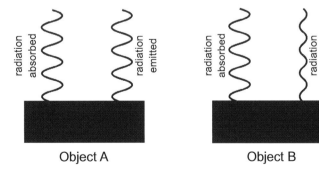

Object A   Object B

Describe what will happen to the temperature of objects A and B over time.

3. The diagram shows how radiation is absorbed and emitted by the Earth.

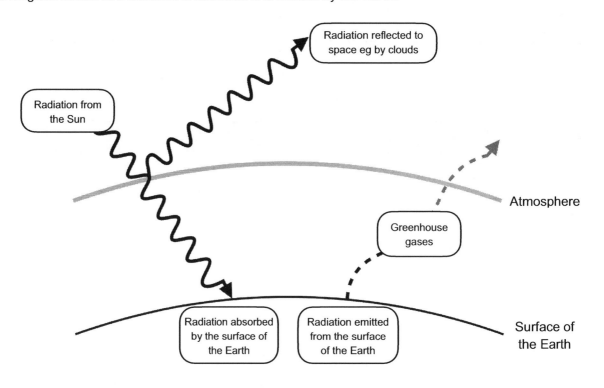

a. Complete the sentences below by using the correct words from the list.

infrared   greenhouse   increase   absorbed   short   clouds   trapped   reflected

The Sun emits _____ wavelength radiation eg visible light and ultraviolet. This radiati

travels through space to the Earth. Some of the radiation is _____ back into space fro

the atmosphere, for example by _____. The remaining radiation passes through the

atmosphere and can be _____ by the surface of the Earth, causing the temperature of

the Earth to_____. The surface of the Earth now emits _____ radiati

However, some of the infrared is absorbed by _____ gases such as carbon dioxide.

As human activity increases the levels of greenhouse gases, more heat energy is _____

in the atmosphere and less is radiated into space. This increases the temperature of the atmosphere.

b. Cloudy nights tend to be warmer than clear nights.
Explain why this is the case in terms of radiation.

Chapter 3 : Magnetism

- Describe the difference between permanent and induced magnets.

- State examples of magnetic materials.

- Describe how to use a magnetic compass to plot the magnetic field of a bar magnet.

- Use the Right Hand Grip Rule to determine the direction of the magnetic field around a wire carrying an electric current.

- Describe how the strength of the magnetic field around a current-carrying wire is affected by the size of the current, the distance from the wire, coiling the wire and using an iron core.

- Describe the advantages of an electromagnet compared to a permanent magnet.

- Describe how a relay and a doorbell both use an electromagnet to carry out their function.

- Describe what is meant by the motor effect.

- Calculate the size of the force experienced by a current-carrying wire in a magnetic field.

- Use Fleming's Left Hand Rule to determine the direction of the force experienced by a current-carrying wire in a magnetic field.

- Describe the role of the split-ring commutator in an electric motor.

- Describe how loudspeakers and headphones use the motor effect to produce sound.

- Describe what is meant by the generator effect and state the factors that affect the size and direction of an induced current.

- Describe how work is done when a magnet induces a current in a coil of wire.

- Describe the differences between an alternator and a dynamo.

- Describe how the generator effect is used in a moving-coil microphone.

- Describe how transformers change the potential difference of an electrical supply and calculate the number of turns or potential difference of a transformer.

- Calculate the input current drawn by a transformer to produce an output power.

- Describe the role of step-up and step-down transformers in the National Grid.

Permanent and Induced Magnets

1. The diagram below shows two permanent bar magnets.

| N | S | N | S |

This shows like / unlike poles near each other.

Like / unlike poles attract / repel.

| N | S | S | N |

This shows like / unlike poles near each other.

Like / unlike poles attract / repel.

a. Draw arrows on the diagrams to show the forces acting.

b. Complete the boxes under each diagram to show what is taking place.

c. Write ✱ at the position where the forces are strongest.

Explain your answer.

d. Explain how the forces experienced by the magnets are non-contact forces.

2. Magnets can be permanent or induced magnets.

a. Complete the sentences below by using the correct words from the list.

| **attraction** | **magnetic** | **permanent** | **magnetism** |

A _____ magnet has its own magnetic field. An induced magnet only becomes magnetic

when placed in a _____ field. If we take away the magnetic field, an induced magnet lose

some or all of its_____ . Induced magnetism always causes a force of _____

b. Object A is a permanent magnet. Objects B and C are either a permanent magnet or an induced magnet.

The diagram shows what happens when these are brought together.

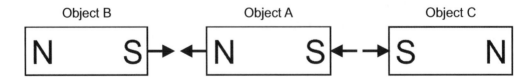

Object B   Object A   Object C

Explain why object B could be an induced magnet but object C must be a permanent magnet.

Magnetic Fields

Some materials can be made into a permanent or induced magnet.

These are called magnetic materials.

Circle the magnetic materials in the list below.

iron   copper   silver   nickel   magnesium   gold   cobalt   zinc   steel

The diagram shows the magnetic field around a permanent magnet.

Several pieces of iron (A, B and C) have been placed into the magnetic field.

These have become induced magnets.

Draw arrows to show the forces acting on the induced magnets due to the permanent magnet.

Explain your answer.

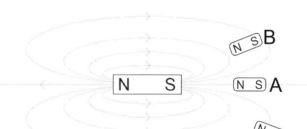

Write the correct word to complete the box below.

> A magnetic field is a region around a magnet where a _____
>
> acts on another magnet or on a magnetic material

Another object was placed in the magnetic field and experienced a force of repulsion.

Explain why this could not have been an induced magnet.

A magnetic compass contains a small bar magnet. We can use this to plot a magnetic field around a bar magnet.

The boxes below show the stages. Place these boxes in the correct order.

Draw an arrow pointing from the North pole to the South pole	Draw another cross at the North pole of the compass	Continue moving the compass until we reach the South pole of the magnet	Connect all of the crosses with a line
Repeat with different starting points around the north pole of the magnet	Place the compass near the North pole of the bar magnet	Draw a cross at the North pole of the compass	Move the compass so the South pole is on the cross

The Earth's core is magnetic. Explain how a compass can be used to show the Earth has a magnetic field.

Electromagnets

1. The diagram below shows simple electrical circuits.

The arrow shows the direction of the conventional current.

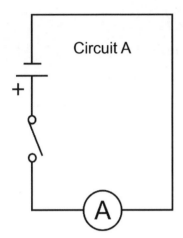

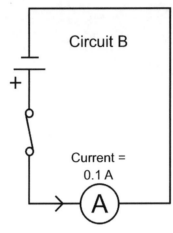

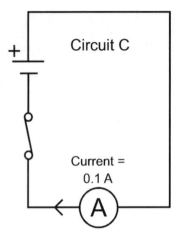

a. What would happen to a compass placed near circuits A, B and C?

Explain your answer.

b. Draw the magnetic fields around the circuits.

c. Complete the box below to show the right hand grip rule.

To find the direction of a magnetic field produced by a straight wire, place your _____

so the _____ is pointing in the direction of the conventional current. The direction

of the magnetic field is shown by the direction that your _____ are pointing in.

---

2. The diagram shows two circuits.

A compass placed near each circuit would deflect due to the magnetic field.

a. Which circuit would produce the greatest deflection in the compass?

Explain your answer.

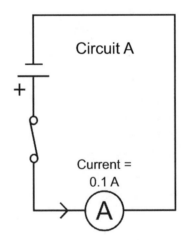

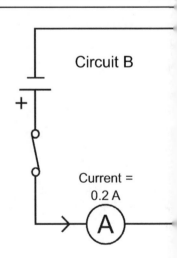

b. Describe what would happen if we increased the distance between the compass and the circuit.

Explain your answer.

. We can increase the strength of the magnetic field by coiling
ᴉe wire.

. What name do scientists give to the coiled wire?

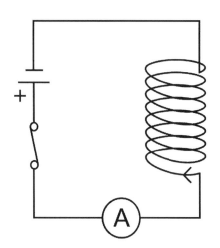

. Draw the shape of the magnetic field produced in the coil.
. How would you describe the magnetic field produced in
ᴉe coil?

. Complete the box below to show how to determine the direction of the magnetic field in a solenoid.

Grip the fingers of your right hand so they point in the direction of the _____ current.

Your _____ points in the direction of the North pole.

Determine the direction of the North pole in the solenoid above.

The diagram shows four circuits containing a solenoid.

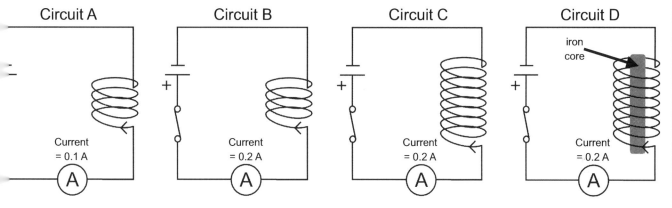

plain the following.

The magnetic field in circuit B is twice as strong as circuit A.

The magnetic field in circuit C is twice as strong as circuit B and four times as strong as circuit A.

The magnetic field in circuit D is the strongest of the four circuits.

A solenoid containing an iron core is called an electromagnet.
scribe two advantages of electromagnets compared to permanent magnets.

Electromagnetic Devices

1. Many devices eg large machines require a high voltage electrical supply.

This is shown in the diagram on the right.

a. Explain why it can be dangerous to turn the high voltage appliance on and off.

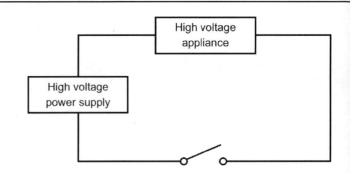

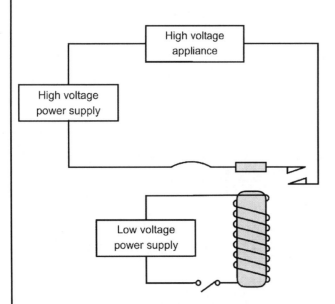

To make the appliance safe, we can use a relay to turn the appliance on and off.

This is shown in the diagram on the left.

b. Label the diagram to show the electromagnet, the spring, the iron block and the contacts.

c. Explain why the high voltage circuit is turned off in the diagram.

2. The diagram on the right shows the low voltage circuit turned on.

a. Describe what happens to the electromagnet.

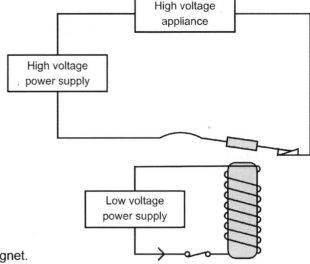

b. Draw the shape of the magnetic field produced by the electromagnet.

c. Use the right hand grip rule to show the North and South poles on the electromagnet.

d. Explain why the iron block is attracted to the electromagnet.

e. What is the purpose of the spring?

. A doorbell is another device containing an electromagnet.

he diagram below shows a doorbell.

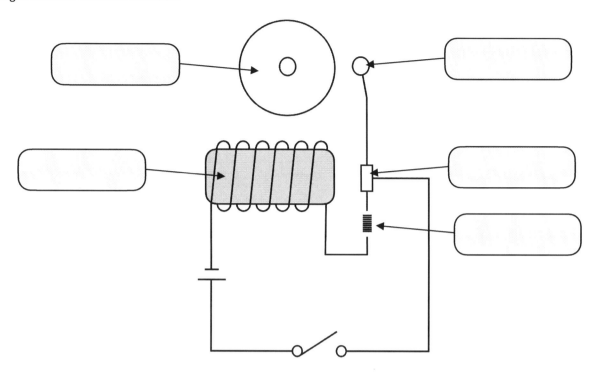

Label the diagram using the labels below.

bell   **clapper**   **spring**   **electromagnet**   **iron contact**

Explain why the clapper is not in contact with the bell in the diagram above.

the diagram below, the doorbell has been pressed and the circuit is complete.

Describe what happens to the electromagnet when the circuit
complete.

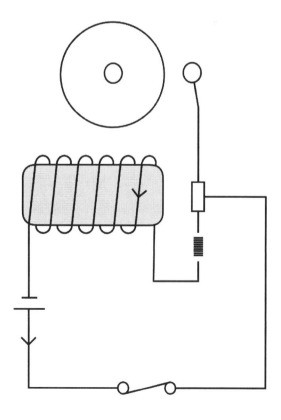

Draw the magnetic field and label the North and South poles.

Describe the effect of the magnetic field on the iron contact.

Explain how the circuit causes the bell to ring continuously
her than once.

The Motor Effect

1. A wire carrying a current experiences a force in a magnetic field. This is called the motor effect.

We can calculate the size of the force using the equation below (you are given this equation in the exam).

$$\frac{\text{Force}}{(N)} = \frac{\text{Magnetic Flux}}{\text{Density (T)}} \times \frac{\text{Current}}{(A)} \times \frac{\text{Length}}{(m)}$$

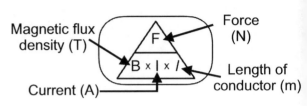

Magnetic flux density (T) — Force (N) — Current (A) — Length of conductor (m)

a. A wire is at right angles to a magnetic field. The wire is carrying a current of 0.5 A and has a length of 0.5 m.

The magnetic flux density is 0.2 T. Calculate the force experienced by the wire.

Force = _____ N

b. A wire is at right angles to a magnetic field. The wire carries a current of 0.2 A and has a length of 1.5 m.

The wire experiences a force of 0.03 N. Calculate the magnetic flux density.

Magnetic flux density = _____ T

c. A wire is at right angles to a magnetic field. The wire carries a current of 0.4 A and experiences a force of 0.1 N.

The magnetic flux density = 0.05 T. Calculate the length of the wire.

Length = _____

2. We can determine the direction of the force by using Fleming's Left Hand Rule.

This is shown in the diagram on the right.

a. Complete the diagram to show the force, the conventional current and the magnetic field.

b. The diagram below shows several wires in magnetic fields.

The arrow shows the direction of the conventional current.

Show the direction of the force for conductors A, B, C and D.

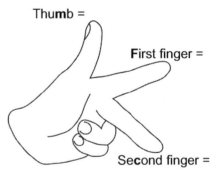

Thumb =

First finger =

Second finger =

Conductor A	Conductor B	Conductor C	Conductor D	Conductor E

c. Explain why there is no force acting on conductor E.

The Electric Motor

xam tip: A lot of students really struggle with the idea of the electric motor. The way to understand this is to always think about the direction of the force on either side of the coil of wire.

. The diagram shows a coil of wire in a magnetic field (note that only the poles of the field are shown).

he arrows show the conventional current.

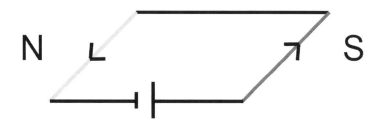

Draw lines to show the direction of the magnetic field.

. Use Fleming's Left Hand Rule to show the direction of the force on the left side of the coil (shown in light grey) nd on the right hand side of the coil (shown in dark grey).

What will be the direction of rotation of the coil?

Clockwise   Anticlockwise

Because of the forces, the coil has rotated by 90°.

his is shown on the left below.

omentum now causes the coil to continue rotating. This is shown on the right below.

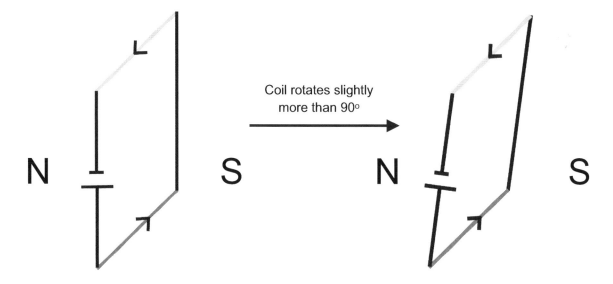

Coil rotates slightly more than 90°

Use Fleming's Left Hand Rule to show the direction of the force on the top of the coil (shown in light grey) and the bottom of the coil (shown in dark grey).

Explain why the coil cannot rotate past 90°.

3. From question 2, we can see that the coil of wire cannot rotate past 90º.

This is because the forces acting on the coil make the coil move back to the 90º position.

To solve this problem, we need to switch the direction of the forces when the coil reaches 90º.

We can do this by switching the direction of the conventional current using a split-ring commutator.

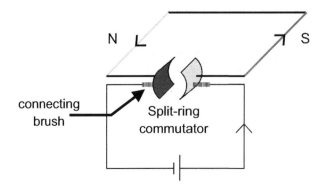

a. Use Fleming's Left Hand Rule to determine the direction of forces acting on the left hand side of the coil (light grey) and the right hand side (dark grey).

Draw these on the diagram above.

The coil now rotates to 90º and the current breaks for a fraction of a second. Momentum means that the coil continues moving. The split-ring commutator now causes the direction of the current to switch.

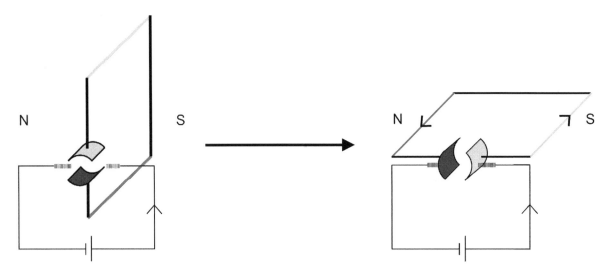

b. Use Fleming's Left Hand Rule to determine the direction of forces acting on the right hand side of the coil (light grey) and the left hand side (dark grey).

On the top diagram, the light grey side had a force acting upwards and the dark grey side had a force acting downwards.

c. Complete the sentences below by using the correct words from the list.

   downwards   **direction**   **clockwise**   **upwards**

The split-ring commutator ensures that the current always points in the same _____ on either side

of the coil. This means that the force on the left hand side always points _____ and the force on th

right hand side always points _____ . This ensures that the rotation of the coil is always in the

_____ direction.

Loudspeakers and Headphones

. The diagram shows a loudspeaker.

. Label the diagram using the labels below.

coil   **cone**   **AC supply**   **permanent magnet**

. Explain how the current in the coil causes the cone to move.

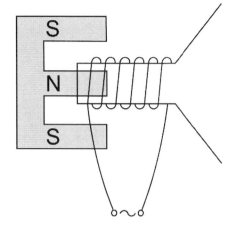

The diagrams below show two loudspeakers.

n each diagram, write the North and South poles on the coil and draw arrows to show the force acting.

omplete the sentences to describe what happens in each case.

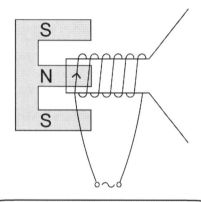

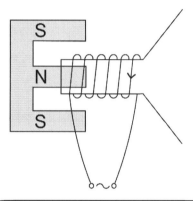

The coil is attracted to / repelled by the permanent magnet

The cone moves inwards / outwards

The coil is attracted to / repelled by the permanent magnet

The cone moves inwards / outwards

A scientist connected a loudspeaker to an oscilloscope and changed the frequency and current of the AC supply.

e traces are shown below. Draw lines to connect each trace to the correct description.

| Low pitch loud sound | High pitch quiet sound | Low pitch quiet sound | High pitch loud sound |

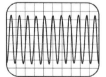

| Low frequency and low current AC | Low frequency and high current AC | High frequency and high current AC | High frequency and low current AC |

The Generator Effect

1. A wire moving through a magnetic field has a potential difference.

This is called the induced potential.

The diagrams below show a wire near a magnetic field.

A

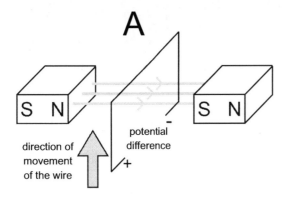

direction of
movement
of the wire

potential
difference

B

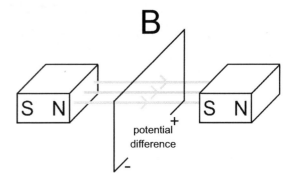

potential
difference

C

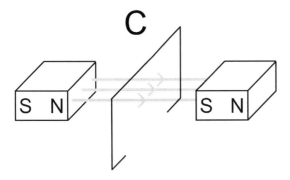

D

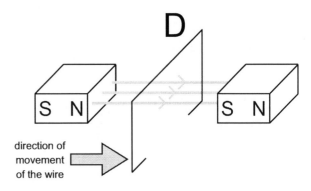

direction of
movement
of the wire

a. Label diagram B to show the direction of movement of the wire.

Explain your answer.

b. Is the wire moving in diagram C?

Explain your answer.

c. Explain why there is no potential difference across wire D.

d. If we move a loop of wire through a magnetic field then we induce a current in the loop of wire.

What do scientists call this?

The induction effect	The dynamo effect	The generator effect

. The boxes below show ways that we can change the size of the induced potential difference and current. Write "+" if the induced potential difference and current increase or "-" if they decrease.

| Change the loop of wire into a coil with 4 turns | Move the wire less rapidly | Increase the strength of the magnetic field |

| Move the wire more rapidly | Decrease the strength of the magnetic field | Change a coil with 4 turns into a single loop |

We can also induce a potential difference and current if we move a magnet in or out of a loop of wire.

ssume that all magnets are the same in the diagrams below.

A
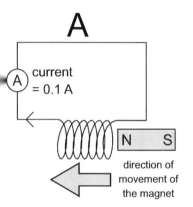

B
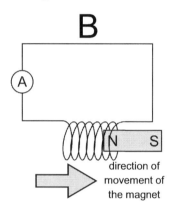

C
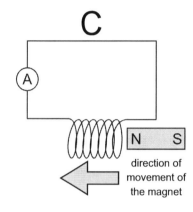

The magnet in diagram B is moved at the same speed as the magnet in diagram A.

etermine the size and direction of the current in circuit B and explain your answer.

The magnet in diagram C is moved at twice the speed as the magnet in diagram A.

etermine the size and direction of the current in circuit C and explain your answer.

Apart from moving the magnet or the coil, how else can we induce a potential difference and current?

When we induce a current in a coil of wire, this causes the coil to develop own magnetic field.

Write the North and South poles on the coil of wire.

What happens to the bar magnet as we push it into the coil?

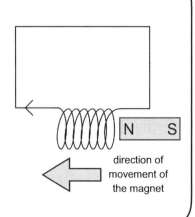

Explain how work is done when we move the magnet in and out of the coil.

The Alternator and Dynamo

1. An electric current can be generated with an alternator. Alternators produce an alternating current (AC).

One side of the loop of wire is shown as a dotted line but remember that this is still a solid wire.

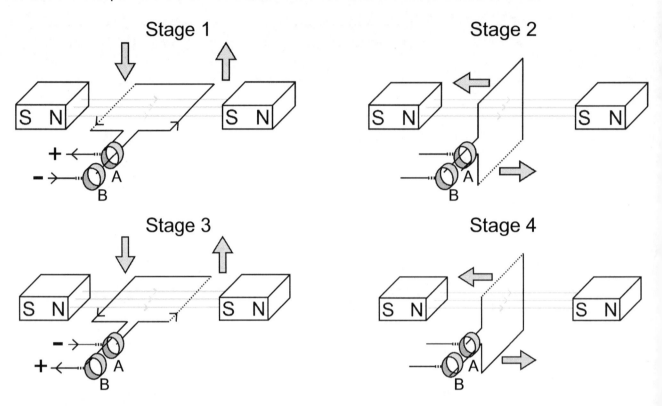

Complete the sentences below to describe the potential difference (p.d.) graph produced by an alternator.

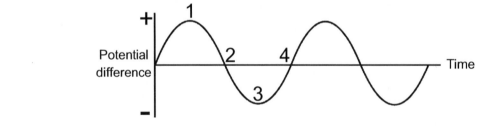

| **A** | **down** | **zero** | **up** | **negative** | **fastest** | **B** |

In stage 1, the p.d. is maximum as the coil is sweeping through the magnetic field at the

_____ possible rate. The side sweeping down connects to ring _____ , making this positi

The side sweeping up connects to ring _____ , making this negative. In stage 2, the p.d. falls to_____

as the coil is moving horizontally and is not sweeping through the magnetic field. In stage 3, the

p.d. is maximum again. However, the side sweeping _____ is now connected to ring B wh

is now positive. The side sweeping _____ is now connected to ring A so this is

now_____ . In stage 4, the p.d. falls to zero again. This produces an alternating current (A

The graphs below show the potential difference produced by three alternators.

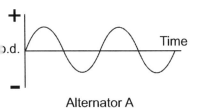

Alternator A

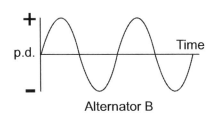

Alternator B

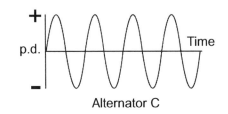

Alternator C

How is alternator B different to alternator A?

(More coils of wire)   (Smaller area of coil)   (Faster rate of turning)

How is alternator C different to alternator A?

(More coils of wire)   (Greater area of coil)   (Faster rate of turning)

The diagram below shows a dynamo. Unlike the alternator, a dynamo contains a split-ring commutator.
The arrows show the direction of movement of the coil.

Stage 1
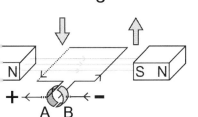

Stage 2
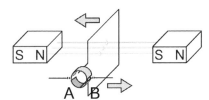

Stage 3
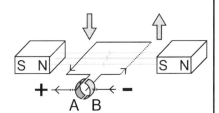

The graph shows the potential difference (p.d.) produced by a dynamo.

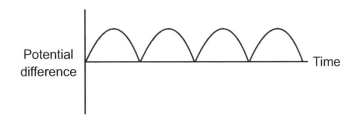

Potential difference   Time

Explain how the graph shows that a dynamo produces a direct current (D.C.).

Label the graph to show one complete rotation of the coil.

Circle the correct words to show how the dynamo produces a direct current (D.C.).

Side A / side B of the split-ring commutator is always connected to the side of the coil moving downwards.

This means that side A is always positive / negative and side B is always positive / negative.

Because of this, the current always flows in the same direction.

The Microphone

1. The following statements are either true or false.

Decide which statements are true and then explain what is incorrect about the false statements.

> The generator effect is used in alternators and dynamos

> The faster the coil of wire moves through a magnetic field, the greater the induced potential difference

> A potential difference is always induced when a coil of wire moves in a magnetic field

> A stronger magnetic field means that a smaller potential difference is induced in the coil of wire than with a weaker magnetic field

2. The diagram shows the structure of a moving coil microphone.

a. Label the diagram using the labels below.

diaphragm   **permanent magnet**   **coil of wire**

b. Describe the structure of the diaphragm.

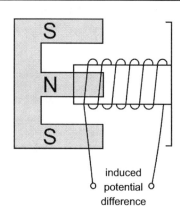

induced potential difference

c. Explain how sound waves in the air induce a potential difference across the ends of the wire.

d. The induced potential difference passes through an amplifier and a loudspeaker. Explain the purpose of these.

e. The diagrams show a cathode ray oscilloscope trace of a sound picked up by a moving-coil microphone.

Complete the traces to show the patterns produced by the sounds described.

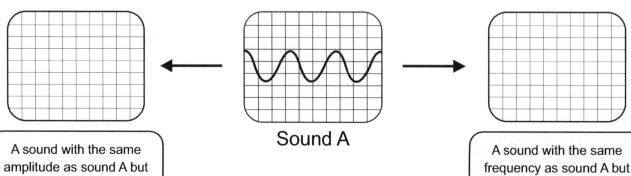

Sound A

> A sound with the same amplitude as sound A but with twice the frequency

> A sound with the same frequency as sound A but with twice the amplitude

Transformers

The diagram shows a transformer.

Transformers are used to change the potential difference of an electricity supply.

Label the diagram using the labels below.

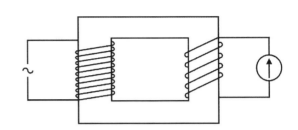

on   output   secondary   primary   AC
ore   coil   coil   supply

Complete the sentences below describing how transformers work.

An alternating current in the _____ coil causes a _____ field.

The _____ core transmits the changing magnetic field to the _____ coil.

The changing magnetic field induces a changing _____ in the secondary coil.

Explain the following:

Transformers have a core made of iron	Transformers only work with an AC supply

For each of the transformers below, state whether a step-up or step-down transformer is shown.

Calculate the input or output potential difference in each case.

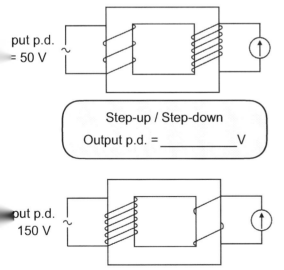

put p.d.
= 50 V

Step-up / Step-down

Output p.d. = _____ V

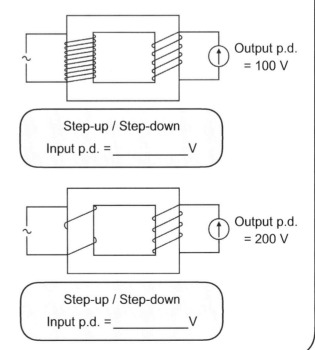

Output p.d.
= 100 V

Step-up / Step-down

Input p.d. = _____ V

put p.d.
150 V

Step-up / Step-down

Output p.d. = _____ V

Output p.d.
= 200 V

Step-up / Step-down

Input p.d. = _____ V

Transformer Calculations

1. We can calculate the potential difference in the primary and secondary coils and the number of turns using the equation below.

You are given this equation in the exam.

Potential difference in primary coil (V)

Number of turns in primary coil

Potential difference in secondary coil (V)

Number of turns in secondary coil

$$\frac{V_p}{V_s} = \frac{N_p}{N_s}$$

a. A transformer has 300 turns in the primary coil and 100 turns in the secondary coil.

The potential difference in the primary coil is 600 V.

Calculate the potential difference in the secondary coil.

b. A transformer has 40 turns in the primary coil and 120 turns in the secondary coil.

The potential difference in the secondary coil is 300 V.

Calculate the potential difference in the primary coil.

c. A transformer has 500 turns in the primary coil The potential difference in the primary coil is 100 V.

The potential difference in the secondary coil is 20 V.

Calculate the number of turns in the secondary coil.

d. A transformer has a potential difference of 1000 V in the primary coil and 100 000 V in the secondary coil.

The number of turns in the secondary coil is 500.

Calculate the number of turns in the primary coil.

If a transformer is 100% efficient then the power of the secondary coil must equal the power of the primary coil. We can use the equation below to make calculations based on power. You are given this equation in the exam.

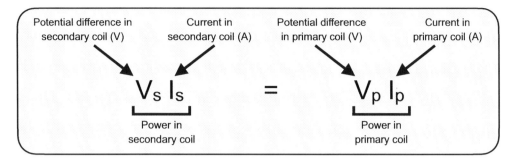

The current in the secondary coil of a transformer is 0.2 A and the potential difference is 50 V.

The potential difference in the primary coil is 25 V.

Calculate the current in the primary coil.

A transformer has a power output of 200 W in the secondary coil.

The potential difference in the primary coil is 40 V.

Calculate the current in the primary coil.

The diagram below shows the National Grid.

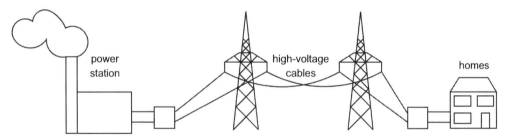

High-voltage power cables transmit electrical power from power stations to homes, factories and offices.

Label the diagram to show the step-up and step-down transformers.

Explain why electricity is transmitted using a high potential difference rather than a high current.

Which of the statements below apply to the step-up transformers and which to the step-down transformers?

Input p.d. is greater than output p.d.	The secondary coil has more turns than the primary coil	Output p.d. is greater than input p.d.	The primary coil has more turns than the secondary coil

Chapter 4 : Space Physics

- State the order of the planets in the Solar System.
- Categorise the planets into small rocky planets and large planets.
- State the location of the dwarf planets and give an example of a dwarf planet.
- Describe what is meant by a moon.
- Describe what is meant by a galaxy.
- Describe how a star is formed.
- Describe the forces acting within a star.
- Describe the lifecycle of stars around the same size as the Sun and stars which are much larger than the Sun.
- Describe what is meant by a geostationary satellite.
- Explain why a body in orbit has a constant speed but a changing velocity.
- Explain why the radius of a satellite decreases when its speed increases.
- Describe what is meant by red-shift.
- Describe what is meant by the Big Bang theory and explain how red-shift provides evidence for this.
- Describe what is meant by dark matter and dark energy and how these could be the reason why the expansion of the Universe is speeding up.

The Solar System

The Solar System consists of eight main planets orbiting the Sun.

Write the names of the planets in the correct order below.

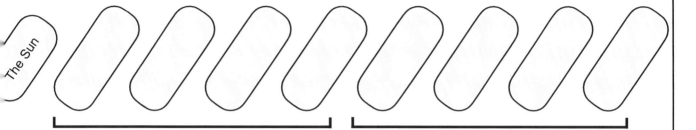

We can divide the main planets into two broad categories: small, rocky planets and large planets.

Write which of these categories each planet falls into in the space below the list of planets.

The above diagram is not to scale. Explain why.

The Solar System also contains several dwarf planets.

Where are the dwarf planets found?

| Between the Sun and the orbit of Mercury | Between the orbits of the Earth and Mars | Beyond the orbit of Neptune |

State the name of a dwarf planet.

The Solar System also contains a large number of moons.

Complete the box to describe what is meant by a moon.

A moon is a natural _____ in orbit around a _____ .

The Solar System is a tiny part of the Milky Way Galaxy. The Universe contains many billions of galaxies.

Describe what is meant by a galaxy.

The following statements are true or false.

Write "T" for the true statements and "F" for the false statements.

| Mercury is a large planet | A galaxy is bigger than the Universe | The Earth is part of the Milky Way galaxy | Pluto is a dwarf planet |

| The Sun is a star | Moons orbit planets | A galaxy is a group of planets | Only the Earth has a moon |

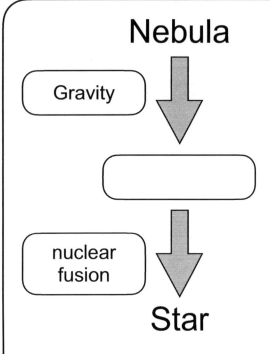

Nebula

Gravity

nuclear
fusion

Star

2. The diagram shows the stages in the formation of a star.

a. Describe what is meant by a nebula.

b. Which is the main gas found in a nebula?

Hydrogen   Helium   Oxygen

c. The force of gravity now causes the nebula to collapse inwards.

Dust particles now move very rapidly.

What happens to the temperature of the particles?

d. What do scientists call the collapsing cloud of hot gas and dust?

Write the name in the space on the left.

e. If the temperature gets hot enough, then nuclear fusion takes place and a star is formed.

Describe what happens in nuclear fusion.

3. There are two forces acting when nuclear fusion takes place in a star.

These are gravity and expansion forces due to fusion energy.

These forces are shown in the diagram.

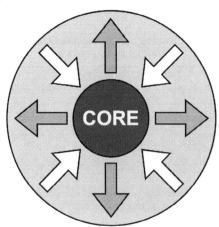

CORE

a. Label the diagram to show the forces acting.

b. When the forces are balanced, the size of the star stays constant.

What name do scientists give to this stage?

Lifecycle of Stars

The lifecycle of a star depends on the size of the star.

The diagram shows the lifecycle of a star around the same size as the Sun. The diagram is not to scale.

Main Sequence Star

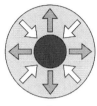

In the main sequence, a star carries out _____ , joining hydrogen nuclei to make heavier elements such as_____ .

The _____ force of gravity is balanced by the outward forces due to fusion energy. The star is in _____ .

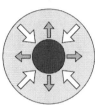

At some point, the _____ starts to run out. Now the outward forces due to _____ are less than the inward force of _____ . The star collapses inwards.

As the star collapses, the temperature of the star _____ .

Now the star fuses together helium nuclei to form _____ elements.

Red Giant

The star now expands to form a _____ . At some point, the star cannot fuse helium and starts to _____ .

White Dwarf

The star now forms a small body called a _____ .

Because nuclear fusion has _____ , this gradually cools down.

Eventually the star cools completely to form a _____ .

Black Dwarf

black dwarf	hydrogen	inward	nuclear fusion	white dwarf	fusion energy	heavier
shrink	helium	red giant	gravity	equilibrium	stopped	increases

2. Stars which are much larger than the Sun follow a different lifecycle. This is shown in the diagram on the left.

a. What triggers the main sequence star to expand into a red supergiant?

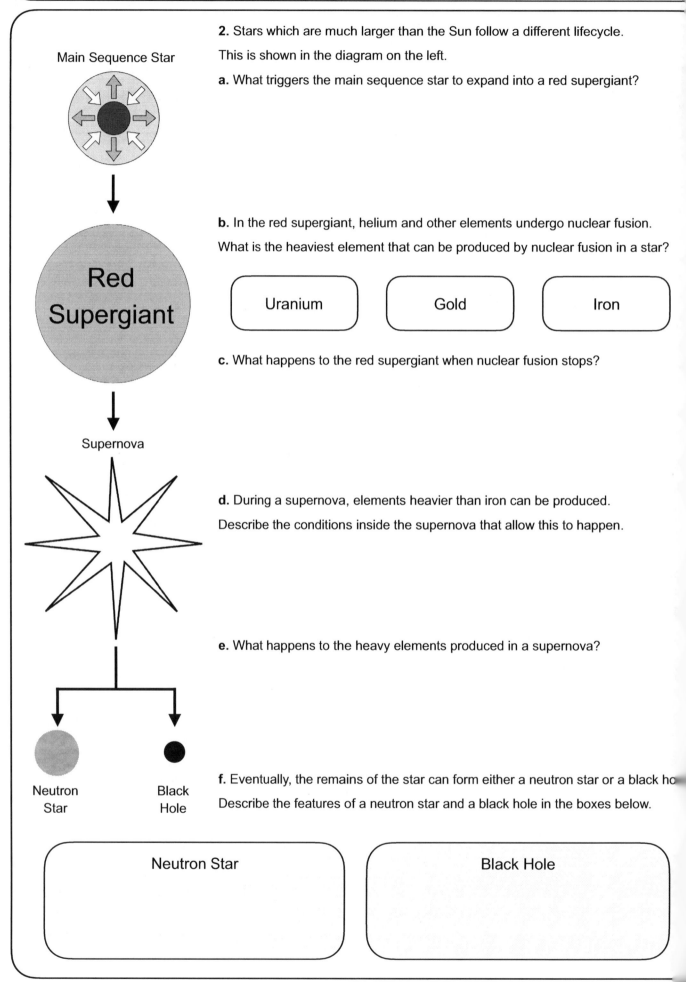

Main Sequence Star

Red Supergiant

Supernova

Neutron Star

Black Hole

b. In the red supergiant, helium and other elements undergo nuclear fusion. What is the heaviest element that can be produced by nuclear fusion in a star?

| Uranium | Gold | Iron |

c. What happens to the red supergiant when nuclear fusion stops?

d. During a supernova, elements heavier than iron can be produced. Describe the conditions inside the supernova that allow this to happen.

e. What happens to the heavy elements produced in a supernova?

f. Eventually, the remains of the star can form either a neutron star or a black hole. Describe the features of a neutron star and a black hole in the boxes below.

| Neutron Star | Black Hole |

Orbital Motion

The diagrams below show three examples of circular orbits. The diagrams are not to scale.

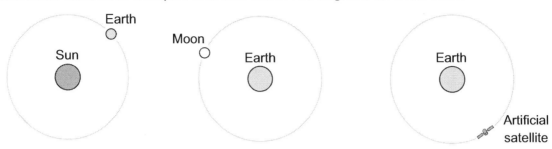

Which force holds these objects in orbit?

Draw arrows to show the direction of this force on the diagrams above.

Satellite TV is broadcast via artificial satellites orbiting the Earth.

Describe the difference between natural satellites such as the Moon and artificial satellites.

The diagram shows a satellite orbiting the Earth.

The arrow shows the direction that the satellite is moving.

The satellite orbits the Earth once every 24 hours.

This means that the satellite always points to the same part of the Earth.

What name do scientists give to satellites like this?

> Polar satellites

> Gravitational satellites

> Geostationary satellites

The time interval between the two pictures is 6 hours.

Explain how the diagram shows that the satellite orbits the Earth once every 24 hours.

Objects in circular motion such as satellites have a constant speed but a changing velocity.

Use the diagram to explain how this is the case.

The diagram shows a satellite increasing its speed of orbit.

Explain why the radius of the orbit decreases as the satellite increases in speed.

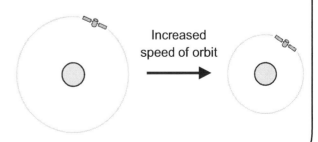

Increased speed of orbit

Red-Shift

1. If we take light from the Sun and pass it through a prism, we get a spectrum.

Scientists noticed that the spectrum contains a number of dark lines. These are shown in the diagram below.

violet end of spectrum
(shorter wavelength)

red end of spectrum
(longer wavelength)

a. Explain the cause of the dark lines.

b. Scientists compared the spectrum from the Sun with spectra from different galaxies.

These are shown in the diagram on the right.

What do you notice about the light from galaxy A?

light from the Sun

light from galaxy

light from galaxy

c. This effect is called red-shift. Which of the following explains the cause of red-shift?

| Galaxy A is moving towards us. The wavelength of light appears to have decreased. | Galaxy A is moving away from us. The wavelength of light appears to have increased. | Galaxy A is not moving. The wavelength of light appears to be unchanged. |

d. Galaxy B is further away from us than galaxy A.

What does the spectrum from galaxy B tell us about how the galaxies are moving?

e. How do the above spectra show that the Universe is expanding?

f. From these results, scientists developed the Big Bang theory. Describe the Big Bang theory.

g. Scientists assumed that the force of gravity would cause the expansion of the Universe to slow down.

However, observations of supernovae show that expansion is speeding up.

How do scientists explain this?

Physics Paper 2

GCSE Specimen Paper

Time allowed: 105 minutes

Maximum marks: 100

Please note that this is a specimen exam paper written by freesciencelessons. The questions are meant to reflect the style of questions that you might see in your GCSE Physics exam.

Neither the exam paper nor the mark scheme have been endorsed by any exam board. The answers are my best estimates of what would be accepted but I cannot guarantee that this would be the case. I do not offer any guarantee that the level you achieve in this specimen paper is the level that you will achieve in the real exam.

1 A student wanted to investigate how the extension of a spring depends on the weight.

Figure 1 shows the student's equipment.

Figure 1

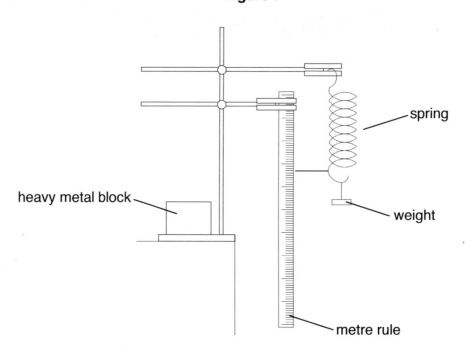

1.1 Describe how the student could use the equipment to investigate how the extension of the spring depends on the weight.

6 ma

_____

_____

_____

_____

_____

_____

_____

_____

_____

_____

Figure 2 shows the student's results.

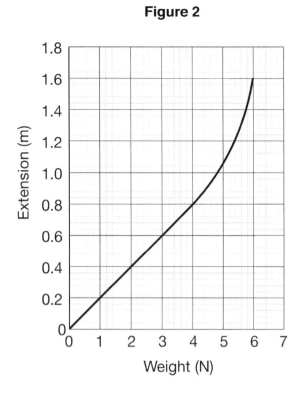

Figure 2

1.2 The graph is linear up to a weight of 0.4 N.

Determine the spring constant of the spring during the linear part of the graph.

2 marks

Use the equation below.

$$\text{Spring constant (N / m)} = \frac{\text{Force (N)}}{\text{Extension (m)}}$$

Spring constant = _____ N / m

1.3 Complete the sentence below.

1 mark

After 0.4 N, we have exceeded the _____ of proportionality.

Total = 9

2   **Figure 3** shows the electromagnetic spectrum.

Figure 3

Radio waves	A	Infrared	Visible light	Ultraviolet	X rays	Gamma rays

2 . 1   Give the name of the electromagnetic radiation shown as **A** in the diagram.

1 mark

_____

2 . 2   Give an example of a type of radiation with a longer wavelength than infrared.

1 mark

_____

2 . 3   Give an example of a type of radiation with a higher frequency than visible light.

1 mark

_____

2 . 4   Which type of radiation causes the skin to age prematurely?

1 mark

_____

2 . 5   Give the name of a type of radiation which is ionising.

1 mark

_____

2 . 6   Complete the sentences below.

2 marks

An electron moves to a higher energy level when electromagnetic radiation is

_____ by an atom.

Gamma rays originate from changes in the _____ of an atom.

We can measure the amount of infrared radiation emitted by different surfaces.

To do this, we use a Leslie's cube. This is shown in **figure 4**.

A Leslie's cube has four different surfaces: matt black, shiny black, matt white and silver.

Figure 4

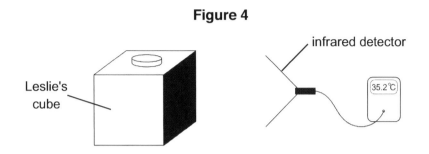

First we fill the Leslie's cube with hot water.

We then use the infrared detector to measure the temperature of the different surfaces.

2 . 7   State the independent variable in this experiment.

1 mark

_____

2 . 8   The infrared detector in **figure 4** has a resolution of 0.1 ºC.

Suggest why we would not carry out this experiment using a detector with a resolution of 1ºC.

1 mark

_____

_____

2 . 9   A student found that the matt black surface emitted the most infrared and the silver surface emitted the least.

How could she determine whether this finding was reproducible?

2 marks

_____

_____

_____

Total = 11

3　　**Figure 5** shows a wave.

Figure 5

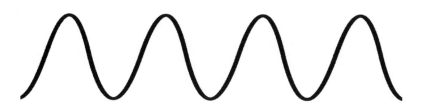

3 . 1　　Complete the sentences by selecting the correct words below.

4 mar

longitudinal　　　　　　**frequency**　　　　　　**transverse**　　　　**amplitude**

The wave shown in **figure 5** is an example of a _____ wave.

The _____ is the maximum displacement of a point of a

wave away from its undisturbed position.

The _____ is the number of waves passing a point each second.

Sound waves travelling through air are an example of a _____ wave

3 . 2　　Label the wavelength on **figure 5**.

1 ma

3 . 3　　The period of the wave is 0.2 s.

2 ma

Calculate the frequency of the wave.

Use the Physics Equation Sheet.

Frequency = _____ H

3 . 4   Describe a method that could be used to measure the speed of sound waves in air.

Your method should include the equipment needed to carry out the experiment.

4 marks

_____

_____

_____

_____

_____

_____

3 . 5   State the equation that links frequency, wave speed and wavelength.

1 mark

_____

3 . 6   A sound wave in air has a frequency of 1700 Hz and a wavelength of 0.2 m.

Calculate the wave speed of the sound wave in air.

1 mark

Wave speed = _____ m / s

3 . 7   How would the sound change if the amplitude decreased?

1 mark

_____

_____

Total = 14

4   This question is about velocity.

4 . 1   Explain why velocity is a vector quantity.

_____

_____

Figure 6 shows a velocity-time graph for a car.

Figure 6

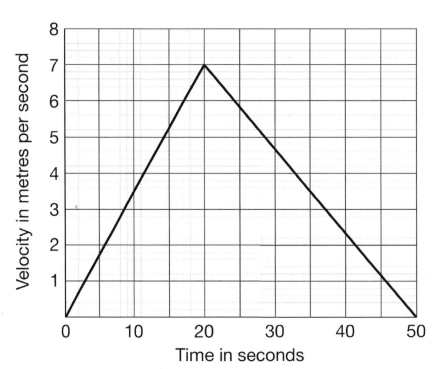

4 . 2   Calculate the acceleration of the car over the first 20 seconds of the journey.

Acceleration = _____ m

4.3   Use **figure 6** to determine the total distance travelled by the car.

2 marks

Distance travelled = _____ m

4.4   When the car decelerated, a braking force of 280 N was applied to the brakes.

The car came to a complete stop in a distance 105 m.

Calculate the work done during the car braking.

2 marks

Work done = _____ J

4.5   Describe the energy transfers taking place when a car brakes.

2 marks

_____

_____

_____

4.6   The braking distance is the distance travelled by a vehicle during braking.

State two factors that can increase the braking distance of a car.

2 marks

_____

_____

_____

Total = 11

5 This question is about magnetism and the uses of magnetism.

5 . 1 Describe the difference between a permanent magnet and an induced magnet.

2 mar

_____

_____

_____

Figure 7 shows a permanent magnet near a magnetic material.

Figure 7

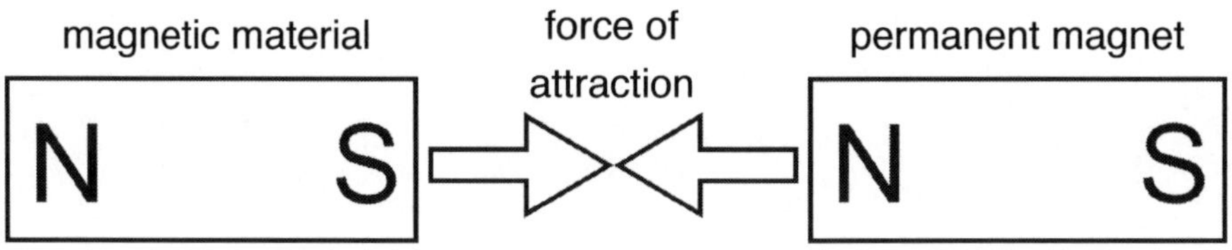

magnetic material   force of attraction   permanent magnet

N   S   N   S

5 . 2 Name a material that could be used to make a permanent magnet.

1 ma

_____

5 . 3 Explain how the magnetic force is an example of a non-contact force.

1 ma

_____

_____

_____

5 . 4 Complete the sentence below.

2 m

The force of attraction is equal in _____ and

opposite in _____ .

5.5   Describe how we could determine whether the magnetic material is also a permanent magnet.

2 marks

_____

_____

_____

Figure 8 shows a wire carrying an electric current at right angles to a magnetic field.

Figure 8

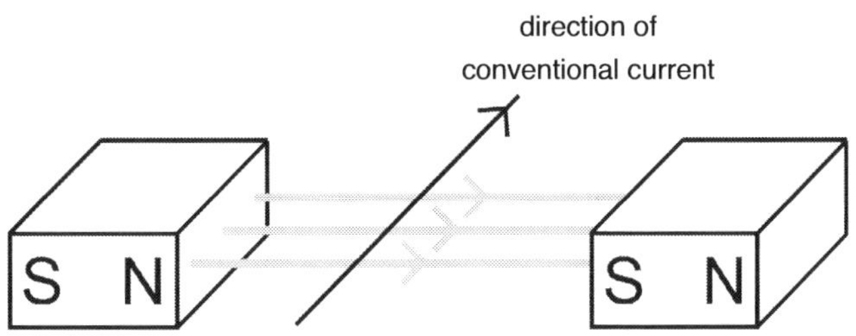

5.6   The wire has a length of 0.5 m and is carrying a current of 4 A.

The wire experiences a force of 0.05 N.

Calculate the magnetic flux density of the magnet.

Use the Physics Equation Sheet.

3 marks

_____

_____

_____

Magnetic flux density = _____

5.7   Draw an arrow on **figure 8** to show the direction of the force experienced by the wire in the magnetic field.

1 mark

Total = 12

6 This question is about forces.

Figure 9 shows a van driving in a straight line at a constant velocity.

Figure 9

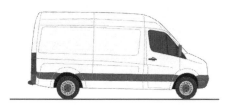

The driving force of the engine is acting in the forward direction.

Resistive forces are also acting on the van.

6 . 1 Draw an arrow on the free-body diagram to show the resistive forces acting on the van.

2 ma

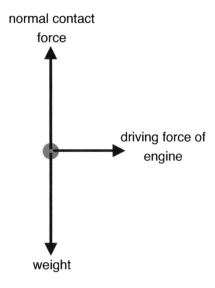

6 . 2 Give an example of a resistive force acting on the van.

1 m

_____

_____

6 . 3   The driving force now increases and the van accelerates.

Complete the sentences below.

3 marks

The acceleration of an object is _____ to the resultant force

acting on the object and inversely proportional to the _____ of the object.

This is Newton's _____ law of motion.

6 . 4   The van reaches a constant velocity of 12 m / s North.

The van collides with a stationary car and both objects move forward together.

Calculate the velocity of the van and car together after the collision.

The mass of the van is 2000 kg and the mass of the car is 1000 kg.

5 marks

_____

_____

_____

_____

_____

_____

_____

_____

Velocity = _____ m / s North

Total = 11

7   This question is about lenses.

Figure 10 shows rays of light passing through a concave lens.

Figure 10

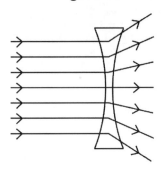

7 . 1   Complete figure 10 to show the principal focus of this lens.

1 ma

Label the principal focus **F**.

7 . 2   Concave lenses can be used to produce an image.

Figure 11 shows a ray diagram using a concave lens.

Figure 11

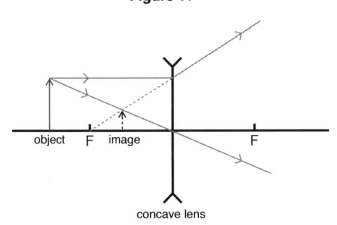

Describe the features of an image produced by a concave lens.

3 m

_____

_____

_____

_____

Convex lenses can also be used to produce an image.

Figure 12 shows a convex lens used as a magnifying glass.

Figure 12

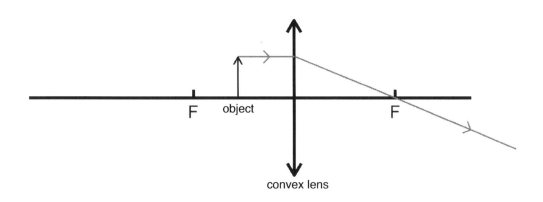

convex lens

7 . 3   Complete **figure 12** to show how the lens forms the image of the object.

3 marks

Use an arrow to show the image.

7 . 4   A person uses a magnifying glass to view an object.

The height of the image produced is 14 mm.

The magnification of the lens is 2.5x.

Calculate the object height.

Use the Physics equation sheet.

2 marks

_____

_____

_____

_____

Object height = _____ mm

Total = 9

8   Transformers are used in the National Grid.

Figure 13 shows a transformer.

Figure 13

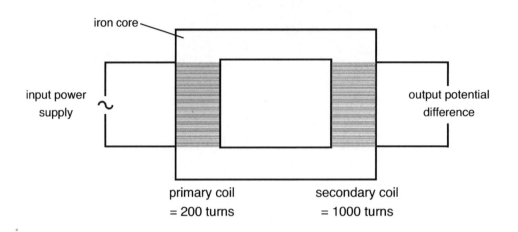

primary coil
= 200 turns

secondary coil
= 1000 turns

8 . 1   Explain why the core is made out of iron.

1 ma

_____

_____

_____

8 . 2   Explain why the input power supply must be an alternating current (AC).

2 ma

_____

_____

_____

_____

_____

8.3   The potential difference across the primary coil was 24 V.

Use data from **figure 13** to calculate the potential difference across the secondary coil.

Use the Physics equation sheet.

3 marks

_____

_____

_____

Output potential difference = _____ V

8.4   The power output of the secondary coil was 240 W.

Calculate the current drawn from the input power supply when the input potential difference is 24 V.

Use the Physics equation sheet.

2 marks

_____

_____

_____

Current drawn from input power supply = _____ A

8.5   Suggest a reason why the power output of the secondary coil may be less than the power input of the primary coil.

1 mark

_____

_____

8.6 Describe how step-up and step-down transformers are used in the National Grid.

In your answer you should explain why these transformers are used.

4 ma

_____

_____

_____

_____

_____

_____

_____

_____

Total

9 The Sun is a main sequence star.

9 . 1 Describe the stages in the formation of a star.

4 marks

_____

_____

_____

_____

_____

_____

9 . 2 Describe the forces acting in a main-sequence star such as the Sun.

3 marks

_____

_____

_____

_____

_____

9 . 3 State the name of the object formed when stars around the same size as the Sun reach the end of their life cycle.

1 mark

_____

9 . 4   **Figure 14** shows the line-spectra of light from the Sun and from a galaxy called M90.

Figure 14

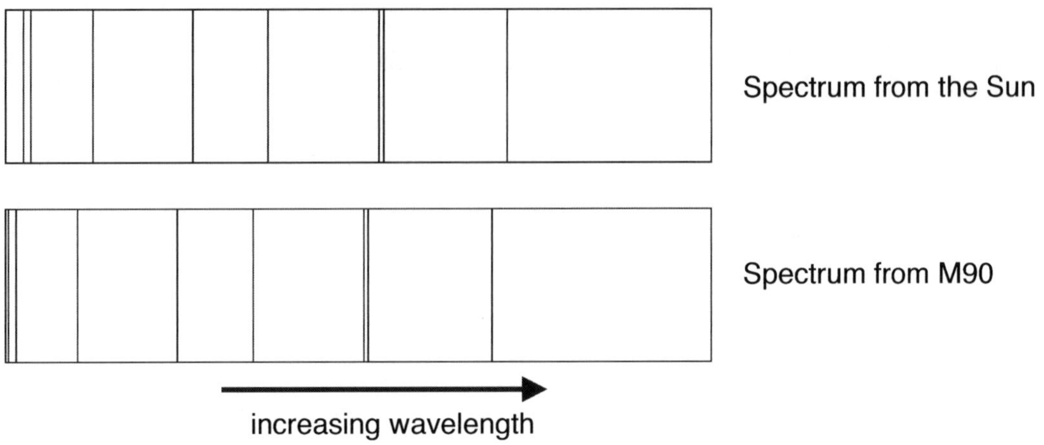

Spectrum from the Sun

Spectrum from M90

increasing wavelength

Explain what these line spectra tell us about the galaxy M90.

2 ma

_____

_____

_____

_____

_____

_____

END OF QUESTIONS

Total

Printed in Great Britain
by Amazon

42332397R00079